# The Secret Science of Modern Martial Arts

Kevin J Mills

Kevin J Mills

© Copyright 2012 Kevin J Mills

All rights reserved. No part of this document may be reproduced or transmitted in any form or by any means, electronic mechanical,
photocopying, recording, or otherwise, without prior written permission of the author, or in accordance with the copyright,
designs and patents act 1988.
Published by Kevin J Mills. PO Box 107, Crediton, Devon, UK, EX17 9AR
ISBN 978-0957604711
For enquiries : spire0951@aol.com

# DEDICATION

To those that seek knowledge and understanding and not just power and ego, to those that want to help and share and not keep and hide, to those with an open mind and heart and not those, with a cold closed mind.

To Leah, Scott and my soul mate Jenni.

## Blackened

Bubbling up through blackened ink and truthful paper,

knowledge bursts through with integrity and honour

seeking out open minds and receptive hearts
and a spirit of kinship no doubt

Within these pages, this journey
awakens a deep desire within

to understand and experience this world,

to seek out meaning and morality
and grasp new wisdom contained with both hands

Leah-Marie Mills

# CONTENTS

Title

Dedication

Introduction

Forward

Acknowledgments

| | | |
|---|---|---|
| 1 | The Refined Science of Stances | 1 |
| 2 | Movement Transition Principles and Propulsion | 11 |
| 3 | Asymmetrical Movement and Speed | 25 |
| 4 | Power Principles of Strikes | 39 |
| 5 | Effective Blocks | 51 |
| 6 | Correct Anatomical Kick Alignment | 63 |
| 7 | Neuromuscular Programming | 75 |
| 8 | Biomechanics of the Body | 85 |
| 9 | Action Reaction | 99 |
| 10 | References | 101 |

# INTRODUCTION

Over a lifetime of training and teaching in the martial arts, I have been fortunate to meet some very talented artists, both in the field of theory and skill, who have helped me improve my art. Yet I have become aware of the difficulty in teaching and explaining the "how" of the execution of a particular physical movement. How does that work? What is going on when I do this or that? Finding the best way to convey your understanding and knowledge to a student can be frustrating. Although we can perform the moves we have practiced all our lives, students stand there and watch the instructor move, then try to imitate those actions, often becoming clones of what they think they see. We explain what we want students to do in words, but we find blank faces staring back at us. These are the innate problems with teaching a martial art.

In the art that I study, American Kenpo, I have been fortunate to have a base code of Principles and Theories that were put in place by its creator, Senior Grand Master Parker (SGMP). This code helps the student understand what goals they are trying to achieve, and helps them visualise the effect of these moves on their attacker. It is my aim within this book to explore these base Principles and Theories and apply them to the human body for their use within the martial arts. I will also add to the thought process that many have begun, using these terms. They are not only specific to American Kenpo in the Ed Parker lineage, as there are many martial arts in the world today that use scientific terms to help students understand what the teacher is trying to convey.

With the onset of more advanced testing tools, scientists are researching and testing the capabilities of the human body. They are going beyond the normal criteria of speed and action and looking into areas such as force delivered, collision affect, damage, stress analysis of joints and muscles, and much more. These I will explore in finer detail as they apply to a martial artist. I will use scientific terms to help us understand why and how moves are designed to work. We will explore the physiology used and the links between what we are thinking consciously and what the mind is doing subconsciously. We will touch on the realms of Neurolinguistic Programming (NLP), as well as Neuromuscular Programming, (NMP). You may have heard the saying, "The devil is in the detail." I take this a step further with, "The devil is in the detail defined." This book will do just that. Why? Because we must remember that there is a difference between our biomechanics and the mechanics of inanimate objects in Newtonian Physics. We cannot take a scientific term and apply it to a block of stone or an iron bar and expect the same result when applied to the human body.

The term must be understood in a different manner. In human biomechanical movement, we deal with a living organism, which registers pain and is capable of learned behavior. We have the ability to move inefficiently but it does not stop us from moving. Mechanical principles that apply to bridges, buildings, cars and planes are generally applicable to the human body, but not always in the same way. The application of these terms and principles to biomechanics and the human body as they relate to the martial arts is what this book is all about.

It is my desire to relay this material in such a way that a martial artist of any style or system may benefit from it. Once you begin to understand the basics, then you will be able to apply it within your own art, with your own interpretation of the principles and theories. After all, we are all built in the same way and we all have the same code, which underwrites our birth and growth. With this said, there are exceptions to the rules. Some individuals can perform feats which defy understanding, but that's only a very small percentage. The majority of us are limited to constraints placed upon us by our physical bodies and its very definable capabilities. We essentially develop in the same way. When we are born, we have no understanding of learned bad behavior, which can put undo strain on our bodies and our health. We all breathe, use our senses, learn to move our limbs, crawl, walk, run and (maybe) fight in the same way.

When we fight, it is usually with no instruction other than our natural urge to survive. As we grow older, something takes over this innate ability to move naturally. We adopt behaviors, which have detrimental effects on our bodies: shallow breathing, lazy walking, and bad posture, for example.

We listen to instructors and fight with moves and strikes we believe to be effective, but we do not understand the importance of our body postures or how our bodies are built to operate and function in an efficient and effective manner. We are not often encouraged to ask questions or push the boundaries of our knowledge and understanding. There are martial arts taught today which are based on a method of fighting from around a thousand years ago. When asked why we do this move or that move, the typical answer is, "That's the way it's done and has always been so." Yet the result of this is often learned bad behavior!

This book will help you get back in touch with efficient body mechanics, and will help you understand that the body is controlled by the mind and is a skillful, powerful and highly complex human machine. We will explore movement in such a way that you will understand that when aligned in the correct manner with good structural support, you will be stronger than you ever thought possible. We will look at mechanisms and ways to think to help you move with speed and purpose, linked with a thought process designed to support your intentions and actions. Through it you will discover a more efficient and effective way of executing your Art. This is what I term NMP—Neuromuscular Programming.

Kevin J Mills

The Secret Science of Modern Martial Arts

# FORWARD

I first met Kevin well over a decade ago. Ed Parker, Jr, who was one of my students at the time, introduced us. Ed is a high character guy and scrutinizes everyone he brings to me. If he shows up with someone, I know they are serious martial artists.

Kevin was a close friend of Ed Parker, Jr. and along with three of his black belts had come to meet and train with some of the Kenpo people in Los Angeles. After twenty years in Kenpo, it was time to find out what the birthplace of American Kenpo had to offer. They hopped in Ed's jeep Cherokee and drove from Pasadena to the Inglewood area of Los Angeles. My school at the time was just off Manchester, where they hung out with me and some of my guys on a training night. I was immediately struck by the seriousness and intensity of Kevin when it came to discussing all things Kenpo. It was obvious that this was not a casual practitioner, but a man with a serious thirst for knowledge. He already owned the Kenpo brick (5th degree) and unlike many others who had come to me for training, he was not looking for rank. "Good," I said to myself. That always makes life so much easier when all a person wants is knowledge. I do not play the rank game. I don't even allow my students to wear it. "Show your rank on the floor and not around your waist" is my motto. We spent the evening talking and sharing; Kevin asked many very well thought-out questions, as did his students. We talked Kenpo philosophy late into the night until Ed had to leave. Kevin and his guys were great, but as usual when I had these types of encounters, I wondered if I would see any of them again. Not just because of the structural differences between our Kenpo styles, Kevin lived and taught in England, so he wasn't exactly in the neighborhood. The truth is I never expected to see him again.

Then the following year something unprecedented happened: Kevin showed up. We spent a great deal of time training and talking Kenpo, as well as sharing many a meal. Another few years went by with Kevin coming over to train with me every several months. One year he showed up with his instructor to meet me. I tell this story so that you will understand the kind of man that he is. Kevin is a man of integrity with fierce loyalty and a driving determination to continue to improve himself in every facet of his life. In his many visits to my home school in Los Angeles, as well as the trips I have made to his home, he and his wife Jenni have never failed to be great students of the art as well as wonderful friends. I cannot say enough about the quality of the person and the intelligence he brings to every project he touches. This book is wholly Kevin's work, a product of his intellect and expression of his knowledge. I hope you get as much out of it as Kevin put into it. It is a labor of love and a work of art. Enjoy!

Ron "Doc" Chapél, Ph.D. Senior Master Professor Sub-level 4 Kenpo

# ACKNOWLEDGMENTS

I would like to thank everyone who has been involved with my journey so far, especially my wife and soul mate, Jenni, who has been through everything and is always there to guide me in the right direction and give encouragement when needed with unending love and support. Thank you for the belief that I can do it, for all the books you purchased for me, and for your understanding of my need to read and learn.

To my children Leah and Scott: each has helped in their own way. Leah for her indomitable humor and wisdom, incredible intellect and her ability to read ever so fast and for her inspirational poems; Scott for all the times when I had to understand the reasons for your growth in character, which ensured that I never stood still, for your inherent intelligence, skill and the time freely given with this project. Also for your support and help in putting together all the video footage and photos used throughout this book, it would not have looked as good without you.

To all my teachers in life, who are also my students friends and family: I have learned so much from you. Sometimes the lessons were hard and often I could not fathom the reason for all the lows and highs. These words would not be here today if it were not for my friend Edmund planting the seed in my mind one sunny July evening. To my instructor Dr. R. Chapel (Doc), who filled my mind and guided me to develop that knowledge. Your understanding of the human body and how it works is beyond most in the field of martial arts. You have pushed the boundaries of understanding and pulled a few lucky souls along with you.

To all my friends and students who have stayed true and supported me in my martial arts journey, I thank you.

The Secret Science of Modern Martial Arts

# 1 THE REFINED SCIENCE OF STANCES

What is biomechanics? There are two close definitions for the study of human movement, kinesiology and biomechanics. Kinesiology is the study of human movement through muscles and nerves within the body. Biomechanics looks at movement through the eyes of Physics, using terms such as "force," "torque," and "levers" to explain and understand movement. It is the application of the Laws of Mechanics applied to human movement. In truth, no book on biomechanics can solely explain our intricate movements; there will ultimately be a crossover of kinesiology into the text. A good understanding of anatomy is required to help analyse certain movements. What I will explore is "Functional Anatomy." This is the study of the components needed to engage and move the body. Biomechanics and Functional Anatomy are entwined.

Let's look at basic stances and how they affect biomechanics, our natural body alignments, and how power is produced from them. Before we do, there is one very important point to cover, and that's the difference in structure between the male and a female pelvic bone. To enable women to give birth, their hips are set wider apart than that of men. This causes their legs to camber in, much like an upturned triangle. Pelvic bones are built to bear the weight of the upper body and to transfer this weight into the lower limbs. Weight bearing down onto the hips of a female with the legs cambered in creates extra pressure which is exerted outward. This very basic mechanical difference means that males have a more aligned lower platform that allows for more efficient movement.

SECTION 1.1

## Natural Stance

The first stance to analyse is the natural standing position. This is also known as the anatomical position, with one small difference. The anatomical position has the palms of the hands facing forward, whereas the natural standing position has the hands turned inward facing the body. It is important that all movement starts from our base position and in this case our natural standing position. This position must be defined to give us a common reference point before we move on to more well known stances, as this stance sets the basis for all that follow. If we get the beginning wrong, then all else which follows is built on bad structure and lack of understanding. How often are we taught in a martial art to stand naturally? The words, "feet together, back straight, shoulders back, chest out, arms by your side," come to mind. These are the classic words spoken to explain what is required from the student while standing to attention. This stance is often referred to as an attention stance, which often requires the feet to be together and touching.

Pic1A - Attention Stance          Pic1B – Natural Stance

Let's look at the human skeletal structure and its basic makeup. If we attach a hook to the skull and lift it in the air, we see the arms and legs dangling beneath the frame. Due to the extension of the shoulders, the arms lie close to the framework, the legs lie directly below the hips without touching, the feet, once placed on the ground, are directly under the legs and the pelvic bone and feet point forward. Pelvic and foot function are directly linked; they affect each other. When we stand straight naturally, our feet face the direction that we are facing. However, what does feet facing forward mean, and how do we know what is naturally correct and what is not? A study of the standing position reveals a vast degree of variances. Some people stand with the feet facing outwards towards 10 and 2 o'clock. Some have heels out and toes in, while others stand with one leg twisted around the other. Over time, this will affect the way they walk, which in turn affects the pelvic function upward into the spinal column. If we can stand correctly, we can walk correctly. Conversely, if we stand incorrectly, our walk and other movement will not be natural or efficient. The feet need to be correctly aligned beneath the pelvic structure; any misalignment will have an effect upon the stability of our stance.

If you take a cast of your foot positions while standing on your feet, you will notice they are slightly curved. This shape often throws your consideration off when you are trying to stand with your feet and hips anatomically aligned. The heels need to be out to ensure that the weight of the body is distributed evenly onto and through the balls of your feet.

Pic2A Horse Stance  Pic2B Wide Horse Stance

The photographs above show that the weight of the body is distributed differently depending upon how far the feet are spread out. This will directly affect the ability to be mobile and move quickly. With the feet below the hips, we are capable of moving the body in just about any direction. While standing naturally, we have a degree of stability, but not as much stability as when the feet are spread as in picture 2A. This stance is labeled the Horse stance. It is the basic training stance for a number of arts. Some are wider as in picture 2B. This latter stance will give a great deal more stability to the upper body, because the centre of gravity is much lower, whereas the Horse stance shown in picture 2A gives some stability with a higher degree of mobility. Part of the stability here is gained from bending the knees and lowering your mass to create a lower centre of gravity. If you stand with your feet naturally apart and bend your knees, you'll notice that if alignment is to be maintained, the knee joint has to work as it is designed as a lever.

The bones form a rigid lever around each joint, (the knee) for example, is a pivot point or fulcrum created around the end of our rigid bone structure. Therefore, the Principle of Levers applies to postures and movement. How far you bend your knees will affect your height. If you over bend and squat, you lose mobility and gain stability. The ideal amount of bend in the knees should not take the knee over your centre of weight distribution point, which is the ball of each foot. When bending, do not allow your knees to part from their alignment with the lower and upper part of your legs; keep an erect back and head.

There is a direct relationship between the shoulders and the pelvic bone. While standing naturally, it is important that your posture be correct. In anatomical terms, the body can be divided into three planes: Median Sagittal, runs from 12 to 6 o'clock, known as "depth"; Coronal or Frontal Plane runs from 3 to 9 o'clock know as "width" and the Transverse Plane, which runs parallel to the ground. The terms width and depth will be used when referring to these planes. These three zones make up our Height, Width, and Depth; they are often found within the art of Kenpo and used as a theory to help understand the martial arts (Parker (1983) vol. 2). If the shoulders are not aligned above the hips, balance and posture will be off. We could also be standing with one shoulder forward and the other back effectively twisting our upper torso. All of these positions will have an affect, not only on our posture but also on our balance. This negatively affects the ability to move and strike with power, speed and effectiveness. The natural standing position should give you an erect posture with equilibrium maintained throughout the body.

Pic3A Fighting Stance incorporating Height, Width & Depth

SECTION 1.2

# THE HORSE STANCE

The horse stance is the most commonly used training stance. In practice, the feet are set wider apart than the pelvic bone, with shoulders back, head upright and straight. Executed in this manner, this is no longer a natural standing position. Some teachings, usually the more traditional, teach this stance for the benefit of training basics. The distance between the feet has been extended, but not as far as the low horse stance shown in the previous Section (Pic2B). It is important to distinguish between the three widths of stances being discussed here. The natural standing position, or natural horse (Pic1B). The horse stance (Pic2A), and the low horse stance (Pic2B), which is just about as wide as you can force the feet apart and still keep the feet pointing forward. It is also impossible in this latter stance to keep the knees and feet aligned, because the feet are beyond the width of the knees. Large amounts of stress are being applied to the knee and ankle joints along the width plane. The majority of the body's weight is forced towards the ground in between the feet, with the knees coming under considerable pressure by forces that push outward toward 3 and 9 o'clock. This wide horse stance will give stability at the cost of mobility and has the potential to do real harm to the lower joints. The horse stance

(Pic2A) shown in the previous section positions the feet just outside the width of the pelvic bone. This position maintains the alignment between the ankles and the knees but not the pelvis; however, it is nowhere near as bad as the wide horse stance. The natural stance (Pic1B) is an anatomical stance aligned beneath the structure of the upper platform; the feet and legs are the support and driving force behind the movement of the body and as such need to be directly under the pelvic bone to ensure effective and efficient movement.

SECTION 1.3

# NEUTRAL BOW FIGHTING STANCE

Let's look at the first fighting position, the neutral bow. There are two positions for the neutral bow: the actual neutral bow fighting stance and a dimensionally accurate neutral bow. There is a subtle difference between them. When using the neutral bow fighting stance, either the left or right foot can be forward. Imagining a line running between 12 and 6 o'clock, place the forward (left) foot to the left of the line with the big toe touching it, while the rear foot has the heel up against the same line, with the feet facing 1:30 on the clock, heels slightly out. From the forward view, we have a distance that is measurable between the two shoulders. This distance is called the "width" of the stance. If your posture is correct, the hips should have the same exposure as the shoulders (Pic4A).

(Pic4A)　　　　　　(Pic4B)　　　　　　(Pic4C)

If you twist your torso and open your shoulders to the front, you would have a wider width at the shoulders then at the hips, and would be twisted out of your natural standing position (Pic4B). The width of a stance has a big affect on being able to produce power. In a side stance, the width between both shoulders and hips is closed (as viewed from 12 o'clock)(Pic4C). In this position, the centre line is hidden from a forward viewpoint and the use of your rear weapons are limited.

The horse stance in comparison allows you full use of all your weapons, while exposing your main centre line targets, with the neutral stance in between the two. Width is determined by how far over the 12 to 6 line you straddle your feet, as seen from the forward viewpoint. Depth is determined by how far apart you place your feet. To be structurally sound, you shouldn't place your feet any further apart than the distance explained above in the horse stance. The feet can be any distance apart from the natural standing stance to the wide horse stance, they will not change the width only the depth and a portion of height. Height is determined by how far apart the feet are, an erect upright posture, and how much the knees are bent. In the neutral stance, centre line targets are protected, with easy use of both front and rear weapons, so it can be viewed as the ideal stance.

SECTION 1.4

# DIMENSIONALLY ACCURATE NEUTRAL BOW

The dimensionally accurate neutral bow stance is virtually the same as the stance in Picture 4A. The only difference is that we need to look at the dimensions of the stance in relation to angles. Picture 5 shows a dimensionally accurate neutral bow stance. The feet point towards 1:30 and are at a 45 degree angle to 12 o'clock, assuming that 12 o'clock is 0 degrees. Both shoulders sit back over the pelvic bone. It is a true dimensionally calculated stance. In later sections, we will look at the movement from a neutral bow into a forward bow. To ensure we are mechanically accurate, we'll use the Dimensionally accurate neutral bow stance (DANBS) to move, rather than the fighting stance in picture 4A. The dimensions of width are accurate, which gives us the right tools to build upon. You may have noticed the horse stance as described in 1.2, has the same dimensions as the DANBS. The only difference is that you are positioned on the 1:30 - 7:30 line, with the head forward. In the horse stance, the head maintains a natural position facing forward, whereas in the neutral bow stance, the head is rotated forward. The degree of rotation needed to keep the head focused forward will depend upon which neutral bow stance is used. In picture 4A, more effort and rotation is needed than in the dimensionally accurate stance. Over-rotating the head may cause unnecessary strain on the fixator muscles.

(Pic5)

SECTION 1.5

# FORWARD BOW STANCE

For the sake of clarity, we will from this point on use the dimensions discussed in 1.4 as our stances base. This will ensure that we adhere to dimensionally accurate positions with mathematical accuracy. In later chapters I will analyse movement from a neutral bow into a forward bow.

(Pic6)

The left foot is positioned forward and set on the diagonal line, (as above) at 45 degrees to 12 o'clock, the same position as a DANBS. The difference is the position of the rear foot. It is also important to look at how we move the rear foot into position, to bring the right hip into play and open up the width of the stance. There are only four ways to move the right foot and re-orientate it so that it faces 12 o'clock. The first two are anatomically incorrect and do not form any part of the subconscious thought process. The two movements are: lifting the ball of the foot and rotating on the heel, or sliding or dragging the entire foot into position. Both of these actions are unnatural movements and we will not perform them. That leaves us with lifting the heel off the floor and pivoting on the ball of the foot, or lifting the whole of the foot off the floor and replacing it in the desired position (Pic6). Assuming a left neutral bow with the left foot to the left of the line and the right heel to the right of the line, the feet are aligned underneath the hips and will face 1:30. By using your width, you rotate around your left hip. This is helped by lifting the heel of the right foot and re-orientating it to face 12 o'clock. This action is the rotational torque element for producing power, which I will cover in more detail later. This in turn brings the right shoulder forward, and by engaging the muscles of the hips, you can bring the right hip around as well.

Now we need to analyse this movement further to really understand what is happening mechanically and what we are trying to achieve with the body. Let's look at the relationship between our hips and shoulders; these four joints are the mainstay of posture and balance.

Their alignment is required for the natural standing stance, where the shoulders are directly above the hips. In the neutral bow, the shoulders should also be above the hips. Imagine a rigid frame connecting the hips to the shoulders moving as one. This visual aid will help you become aware of your posture and weight distribution as we explore movement in more detail.

Now, let's get back to rotational torque and the pivot. In order to have an erect posture with proper weight distribution, we need to ensure that the rigid framework between the hips and shoulders is maintained when we move from one stance to another. Going back to the explanation above, I described the right foot movement from facing 1:30 to face 12:00, and by doing this we bring the hips into play. While weight distribution is directed into the ball of the foot, it is mechanically sound to lift the heel and pivot on the ball of the foot, moving the heel from its 7:30 orientation to 6:00, pointing the foot towards 12 o'clock. Remember, this is all being done in a stationary stance. You have to force the left hip around as you stretch your left leg, moving your heel in the opposite direction than the upper body. If you make no effort at this point to transfer weight forward, you will continue to maintain equal weight and move your upper torso backwards. This creates a problem with your mind's intended action. Your mind is telling you that this action is designed within the martial arts to launch a weapon forward. Instead of backing up this weapon with mass traveling forward, you are actually splitting your force, and as a result, you do not have what can be termed "backup mass". You have no Directional Harmony (Parker, jr. (1992) Encyclopedia of Kenpo), and therefore are unable to execute your move at optimum efficiency.

To ensure that your body is working in tandem with your thoughts and to create anatomical alignment, the rear foot has to be lifted clear off the ground and replaced in a new position facing 12 o'clock, while at the same time you must shorten the distance between your feet. If the forward front foot does not move, this means that the rear foot travels forward, allowing the hip and shoulders to come into alignment, while at the same time allowing your mass to shift. This means that you can load the forward foot with more weight than the rear foot 60% on the forward foot, 40% on the rear. You will have achieved what your mind has intended, and you will have used backup mass, creating directional harmony with your body and weapon.

It is important to ensure that the left hip, which has become the pivot point, does not move rearward when making this transition. Once you have lifted the foot and re-orientated it to 12 o'clock, you will be settled into a dimensionally aligned forward bow stance. The feet are kept in line and underneath the pelvic bone. It is important to maintain this relationship when moving. Imagine the feet are set on two parallel lines running from 6 o'clock to 12 o'clock. If a foot is moved forward, you must ensure that it stays on track and does not move off this line.

## SECTION 1.6
# REVERSE BOW STANCE

This stance is a reverse of the forward bow described in 1.5. Instead of the rear foot moving to create the stance, the forward foot pivots in a similar manner to the above movement. From the dimensionally accurate neutral bow, lift the forward left heel off the ground, pivot on the ball of the foot and re-orientate the foot to face 4:30. The foot moves to a 45-degree angle. The difference here is the forward foot moves clockwise to its position (Pic7), whereas in 1.5, the right foot moves counter-clockwise. As this action is completed, the weight transfers to the right leg, settling with 40% on the front leg and 60% on the rear, the opposite of the Forward Bow. The major difference with this stance is that your intention is to move backwards, if you pay attention to this movement, it will feel relatively stable. This is the same movement as the forward bow, but you will not be able to dimensionally align your body due to the heel moving away from you. If however, you lift the foot and replace it as described in 1.5, you will in effect be trying to move backwards while still maintaining your head position facing forwards, and this will feel very unstable. It is not a natural move, and although it can be trained, is not an efficient movement.

Conclusion

In all the above stances, I have excluded the arms, as my intention is to focus on the alignment and posture of the body in relation to the feet, hips and shoulders. This ensures that the student becomes aware of the posture, alignment, and dimensions required to understand the difference between fighting stances that are both dimensionally accurate and inaccurate. The transitions discussed are the start of the thought process to begin moving the body. The human body has evolved into an efficient machine, moving in the direction we face naturally, forward. We do not have races running backward, as it is not anatomically correct. Our feet are the mechanisms that propel the body; they do not work efficiently moving backward. When we practice the forward and reverse stances, which require making a transitional movement, the stance going forward will always be aligned, whereas the stance going backward will not. I have also created a reference point in the natural standing position, to identify the importance of alignment within the body, to make you aware of your posture, and the fact that the body is asymmetrical.

(Pic7)

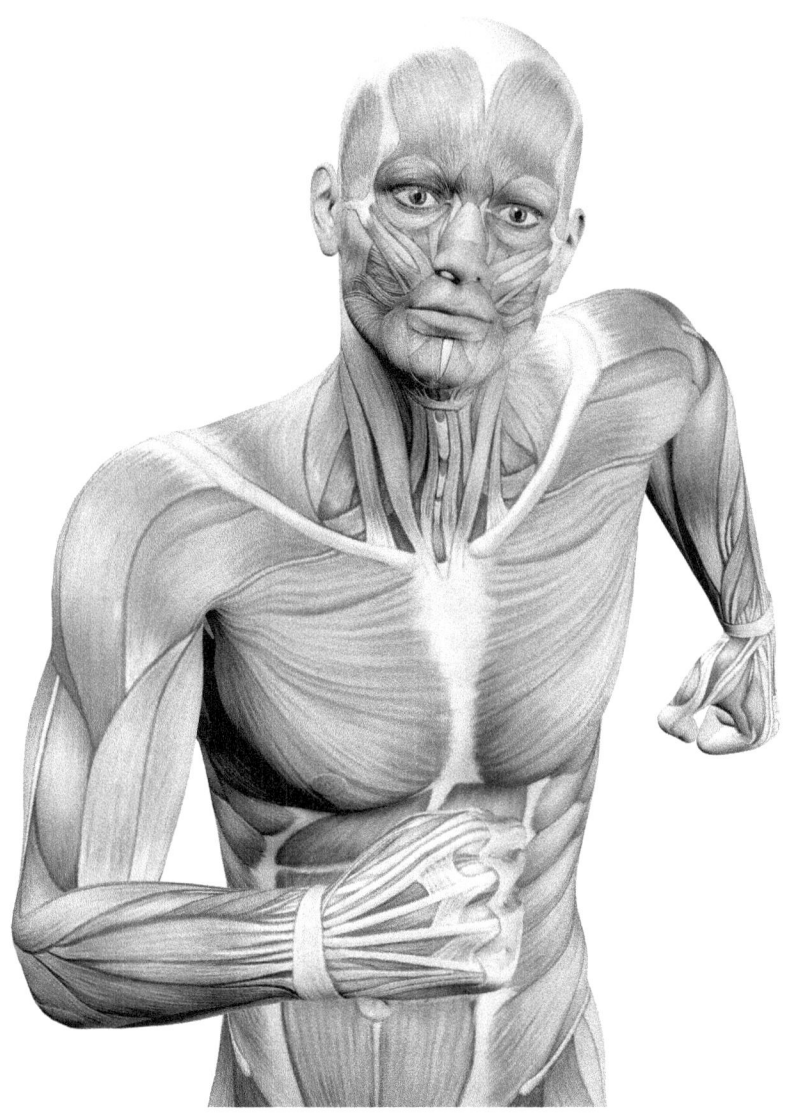

# 2 MOVEMENT, TRANSITION PRINCIPLES AND PROPULSION

One of the most important factors to remember when looking at movement and stance work is that we are all built and made to move the same way. Our feet are aligned directly beneath our hips; therefore when moving we should maintain this relationship.

Imagine that you are standing on two parallel tracks when walking in a straight line, and each foot stays on their own corresponding track. The above pictures show a frontal view of a walking figure with the line helping to indicate two tracks that are aligned to a walking gait. In sport, the record time in the 100-meter sprint has become a sought after record of achievement. Top athletes constantly attempt to break the 10-second barrier. Yet one race that we don't have is the 100 metre sprint backward. The reason is because we are not designed to move efficiently in that direction. Although the body is capable of performing this maneuver, it is not anatomically efficient. This is also true in any martial art when stepping back into any stance.

Let's test what I mean: with the feet positioned underneath the hips, take the left foot and step back towards 6 o'clock. Ensure that when you place the left foot on the ground, it anatomically takes up a position facing 10:30. The right foot maintains its position until the left is settled into position. Once this is done, rotate the right foot in place and ensure that it is solid on the ground parallel with the rear foot. Both feet will now be aligned toward 10:30. Keep your head focused forward to 12 o'clock, and when moving, allow your body to rotate beneath your head. Your head is like a gyroscope. It contains two of the main subsystems of proprioception that move the body and maintains equilibrium when moving. These are the vestibule and visual system.

Proprioceptive senses will be discussed later.

Experiment 1:

Have someone cross his or her arms and perform the maneuver described above. Once they have settled into the stance, place both hands on their shoulders and gently apply pressure front to back, trying to push them out of their stance. Do not jerk, just apply constant pressure. You should notice that the upper torso moves first, followed by the lower platform, until they both move. At this point, we need to analyse the stability of our stance when moving backwards. The body is not designed to move rearward efficiently. The mechanism used to counteract this buoyancy is made up of two systems working together: our movements and the thoughts used to direct those movements. Neurolinguistic Programming (NLP) means the use of words to influence our thoughts. Our postures and movements also influence our mind. This is Neuromuscular Programming (NMP). If we think one thing and then perform a posture that does not support this thought, the body and the mind are discordant. Because of this, we will not be able to perform at optimum efficiency. Just as we can listen to words and be influenced in our actions, so our body can influence our mind and help create, or break down stability, resulting in either a negative body posture, or one in which we are buoyant and easily moved. Negative body posture is shown in the first experiment. We need to create the correct body posture that compliments the action that our mind has asked our body to perform. This is called a Platform Aligning Mechanism (PAM), (Chapél, (1991) course book, S-101 Y).

Therefore we need to create a link between your body and mind. To do so, we raise our forward foot off the floor and firmly replace it in exactly the same position PAM. This will then align our lower platform with our upper platform. As much as our mind creates the correct NMP, our biomechanical movement also plays an important role.

When we lift our heel and foot off the ground and replace it as if moving forward, the whole body has to work to support this action, we are in effect preparing to move forward, so we must engage the rear foot, our calf, thigh and buttock muscles, they all become active in solidifying your stance. After we have taken a step backwards, the coming together of our thought process and our mechanical movement all ensure that the PAM creates a stable base. The moment we create this stability, we become firmly planted on the ground. We are now capable of using the weapons of our upper platform. The difference is they are now being launched from a much more stable base.

Experiment 2:

Have someone cross their arms and repeat the movement described above, but this time include the PAM as described above. Repeat the push with the same intensity, you will find that the body becomes rooted to the ground and becomes much harder to move. In both tests, keep the head erect with good upper body posture and the arms crossed. The only difference between the postures should be the inclusion of the PAM. The above pictures show a Neutral Bow (with the middle picture showing the lifting of the forward foot off the ground).

Throughout our normal activities of daily living, we use natural body movement and postures without thinking about them. For example, opening our hands and positioning them to push a door, walking up stairs, or grasping an apple, are distinct postures. Each of these moves can be attributed to an action that is used within the martial arts, however we do not pay any attention to them, because our mind and body work as one. The autonomic nervous system controls a portion of the body's movement, but body postures are programmed over a lifetime. They tell the mind what it expects to happen. In the explanation above the PAM is the link. We will look at the links between NMP and our postures in more detail later.

SECTION 2.2

# STEP THROUGH FORWARDS

Now that we have created the step back and a stable neutral bow, let's look at movement and propulsion forward. There are so many ways that we can move from one stance into another that we need to settle on the basics first. Martial arts in general will teach all manner of ways to step through forward. For example, a large C step (or zigzag) by touching one foot to another as you move, is a common practice. Let's look at moving from a right neutral bow into a left neutral bow by stepping through forward. When walking in a normal fashion, it is important to pay attention to gait. Over time we may have slipped into many improper habits of walking. If we take time to analyse our own gait, and those of others, we will become aware of the different methods that some employ to walk, yet consider it natural. Pay particular attention to the positioning of the heel followed by the ball of the foot, many have allowed their hips and lower platform to become lazy. Designed as we are, we should maintain the alignment found in the correct anatomical position. The ball of the foot, heel, knee and hip should be relatively in line, allowing for anatomical variances.

The following pictures show a walking figure with feet splayed out to the side.

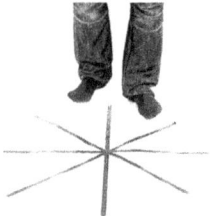 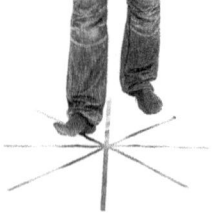 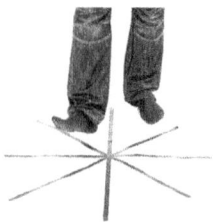

This anatomical gait can be relearned, but it takes time and effort. To start, we first have to ensure that we are aligned while in a neutral bow. To move from one neutral bow to another, we have to change our position to ensure that the move is biomechanically sound.

First, re-orientate the feet to face the direction in which you are stepping. This means moving the feet from their 10:30 alignments to 12 o'clock. To accomplish this, transfer weight to the balls of the feet so you can pivot with ease. In doing so, the hips and pelvic bone become aligned. Momentarily, this creates a different stance called a transitional forward bow, or a mobile forward bow. When this movement is completed, engage the rear leg to push off the ground and move the mass of the body forward. Weight is transferred into the ball of the foot and then onto the stabilising forward foot as the swing of the rear leg occurs. In normal walking, you would place the swinging leg's heel to the floor first, regaining stability at this time. At a slow walking pace, you will always be in a state of stability; as your speed increases, so the need for equilibrium of the body comes into play as the amount of time that you have two feet on the floor decreases. As the swinging leg plants, place it back to the 1:30 alignment, then lift the rear foot and realign it to the same 1:30 alignment. We have now moved from a right neutral bow into a left neutral bow stance. This time the rear foot is creating the PAM. Be careful that the foot does not move backward, as this will send the wrong signal to the brain. You should now be in another stable neutral bow.

The following Pictures show each stage of this step through. Notice that both feet are pivoted to face forward and in doing so create the correct alignment necessary to transition through your step.

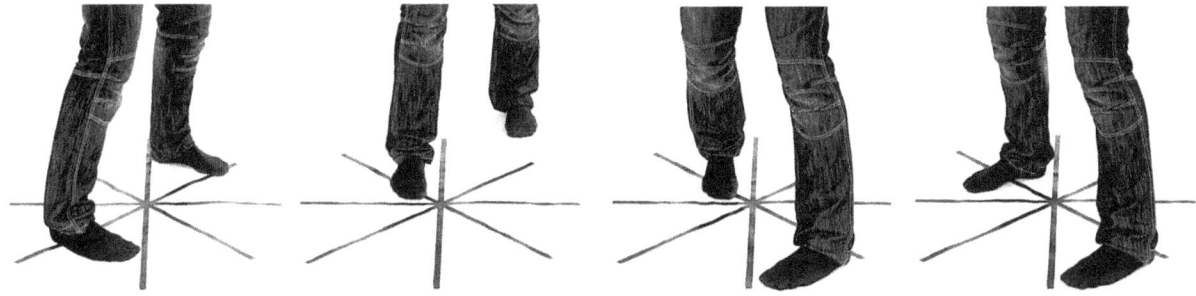

Stepping backward is a reverse of the above explanation for stepping forward; the only difference is that the front foot does the PAM when stepping backwards. It is more important to execute the PAM when stepping back because this movement is a lot less stable than moving forward. This is due to the simple fact that for most of our lives we have been moving forward. It is the natural direction we move in.

SECTION 2.3

# PUSH STEP

The push step (Parker (1992), maneuver is performed while maintaining the neutral bow stance. It can be done while in either a left or right neutral bow stance.

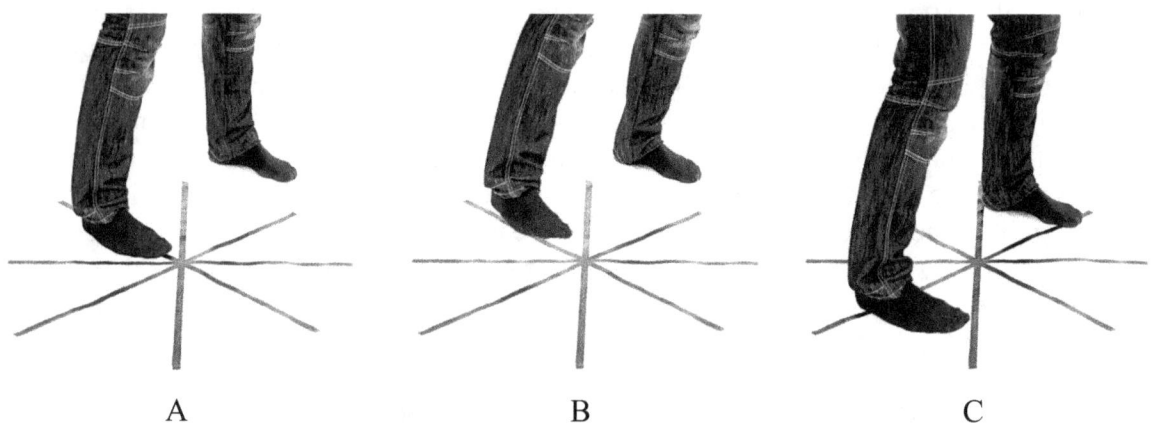

A        B        C

From a right neutral bow stance with the feet aligned as previously discussed, lift the right foot off the ground, picture B above, engage the muscles of the supporting left leg, and push forward. Maintain the alignment relationship as you perform this maneuver; your forward foot plants forward on the ground and is followed immediately by your rear foot PAM. There is a point within this maneuver when both feet are off the ground. This is a major difference between the other two maneuvers in this family, the drag step and the step drag, which each cover a half pace measurement and all maintain the same relationship with the feet. It should not be used to cover great distances, but only used in short controlled bursts of movement of about 150 to 200 mm. Ensure that the same alignment that you started with has been maintained.

SECTION 2.4

# DRAG STEP FORWARD

The very first issue is the description of a drag step, Parker (1992), as it infers that one foot will drag along the floor. This has to be addressed now before bad mechanics set in and you start to move in a learned bad behavioral way. You may already be dragging your feet and need to unlearn this movement. The term "step drag" therefore is very misleading since most people reach the conclusion that "drag" means you must drag or have your foot in contact with the ground to execute a drag maneuver, this is incorrect. The term "drag" derived from the action of the appendage being moved, being behind the direction of travel, because it is being "pulled" or "dragged" behind from the direction that you are moving in.

Let's look first at whether this is a natural body movement and at the effects created on the frame when moving in this manner. The only time that we would have to drag our feet would be if we had injured one of our limbs. Other than that, there is no reason for us to move in this way. When we do, we create friction with the ground and this has an effect of misaligning the body's platform. Over time, this damages the hips and joints of the lower limbs. It also slows movement. An analogy is lowering an anchor over the side of a speeding boat; it slows the boat through friction or "drag". With the right foot forward lift the front foot clear off the ground PicB push off the rear foot and create another neutral bow with your right foot still forward PicC

The drag step will always maintain one foot in contact with the ground at all times. This is executed by moving the rear foot first, forward while maintaining the natural heel and toe alignment. It does not travel beyond a shortened neutral bow stance. What the footwork does is simply shorten the stance, then elongates it to create forward locomotion, as a "shuffling." Once the rear foot has been planted on the floor, lift the forward foot and move it forward the same distance as you moved the rear foot to maintain stance consistency. To create stability, lift the rear foot and PAM it immediately after the forward foot has been placed on the ground. You must maintain functional distance between your feet and the same heel-toe alignment of your neutral bow. The pictures below show the breaking down of this drag step (or step, step, rear foot steps first). After you have moved your rear foot, ensure that you maintain your height while in this transitional stance.

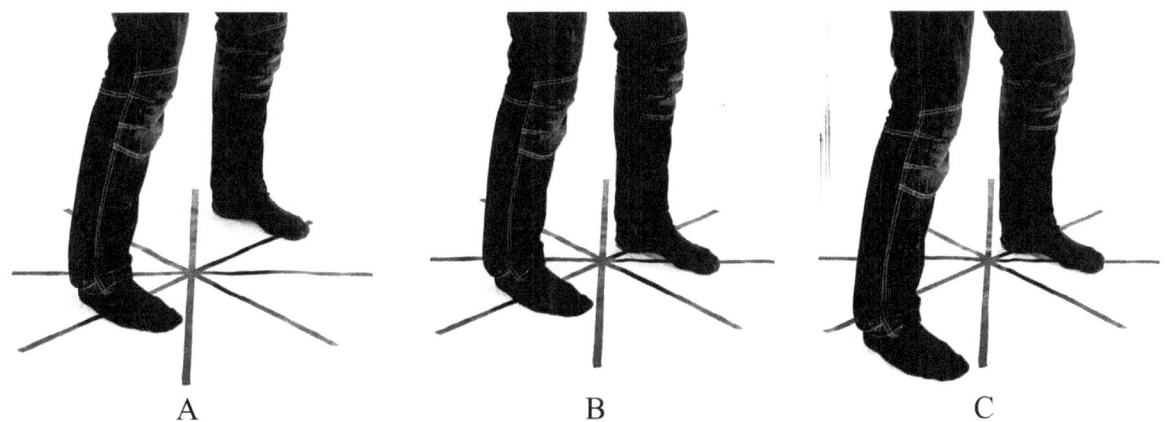

A                               B                               C

This footwork is very useful when moving quickly toward an attacker. The rear foot, moving in the manner described, creates stability to drive the forward foot and in doing so, propels the body's mass forward. The rear leg provides the power at this time, and if contact is made with another force before planting the forward foot to the ground, then the rear supporting leg can be used as a post to power the body into the mass.

This will ensure that any technique can continue to its intended outcome. It is also important to consider that the lower platform, moving in time with the arms and upper platform will be able to maintain a certain amount of timing and rhythm. It is very easy to say, "Your arms should not work faster than you can move your feet." However, the reality is somewhat more difficult.

There are several different ways timing can be altered when executing this maneuver. Take a basic technique as an example and look at how it can be delivered at different stages of our movement, creating a different timing signature, this will also affect the rhythm. Let's use an outward back fist as an example. Using the back of the clenched fist as a weapon, delivered in a fast snapping action, extend the arm and then return it quickly.

The pictures below show a back fist from its pre prepared position out and back to a target say side of the head.

The base starting position for the following move is a right neutral bow, using a right back fist as our weapon of choice; I will explain three different stages when the backfist can be used within the drag step footwork without sacrificing efficacy. As you move the rear left foot forward and plant it half way between your stance, you may execute the back fist at the same time that the foot plants. The intended timing is that when the foot hits the floor, the fist hits the target. You may also delay the back fist until the right forward foot hits the ground. Move the rear left foot in, plant it, push off the same foot, at the same time as the right foot hits the ground execute the backfist. You may delay the fist even further, waiting until you PAM the left foot. I suggest you experiment with the above to try to find which timing signature best meets with the effectiveness of your foot maneuver, in this case the drag step.

## SECTION 2.5

# PROPULSION

We know that our muscles support our skeletal frame and that they are used to move our body. Let's look at the biomechanics used to start movement, the reasons for it, and how it can be used and understood to improve effectiveness. There are two major requirements of stance work. We are trying to create stability from which to strike and have mobility and speed from our footwork to move our body. We have already examined how stability can be obtained at a precise moment, but now we need to look at mobility and speed.

To enable us to understand footwork, let's look at a 100-metre sprinter and how he launches himself from a standstill to a full sprint in a matter of moments. To enable this high acceleration, a sprinter has to have a platform from which to launch his mass. This is accomplished through the alignment of the feet. Our stance in preparation places us in a position where we are ready to engage all our muscles and start as quickly as possible. Just before the launch, rise up so that all the pressure is on the balls of both feet. This further engages our calf muscles to help with the push. Remember the ankle is a true hinge joint, and at this point, the feet use that hinge effectively.

The next question is how can this explosive movement be created without artificial help? The answer lies in how the body instinctively moves from a walk, or a standing position, to a full sprint. In very simple terms, we used what is known in Sublevel 4 Kenpo as a "skip." Chapél (1991). Skipping footwork for speed is one of those natural mechanisms that we use but simply don't recognise because it's so natural, we don't even notice we're doing it. The trick is to be able to study, analyse, and adapt this mechanism for use within the martial arts.

Let's look first at how we use a skip to propel our mass forward fast. While standing still with the feet aligned under the pelvis, we have three ways in which to start moving forward:

A) Engage the muscles and lean forward until gravity takes over and we begin to fall, we then place one foot in front of the other and continue to move, becoming an inverted pendulum.

B) Engage the muscles of the lower limbs by bending the knees and pushing off from a standing position (this can also be performed as we lean).

C) Take one foot and place it behind you as if you were stomping the ground.

This skip mechanism has an effect of propelling the body forward. Let's experiment with this mechanism to bring it into our cognitive thought process. You will discover that you do not need to move the foot very far; you just have to engage the muscles of the calf, place the ball of the foot down first, extend your calf muscle, and allow the natural spring within the ankle to fire your mass. After a short period of purposeful practice, this should become a conscious movement, and speed your initial movement greatly. Now that we have described the skip that propels the body forward and found that it really helps us move, we now understand that to move forward we may skip in the opposite direction to that which we are intending to move. This biomechanical mechanism may also be used in any direction. If you move backwards, you first skip forward to propel the body backwards. If you move to your right from a standing position, you first skip with the left foot to your left and then move to the right. All of these will improve the speed of your initial movement.

These skips are also used if you want to move your body against a mass or force applied by an attacker. To understand and feel this, here are some experiments.

Experiment 3:

While standing in a natural standing position, have someone apply constant pressure to the centre of your back. Once you feel the force being applied, and without moving your feet, try to push and move in the opposite direction of the force being applied. You will find it impossible to just lean into the force and move. Repeat the first part of the experiment above, when force is being applied, "Skip" one of your feet forward, and use this new braced position to push back against the force. The pictures below show the push experiment using the right skipping foot, which helps drive the body backwards against force. You will find that you are capable of exerting pressure, because you have a base from which to push. This experiment can be repeated from either the left or right side or from the front, it works in all directions. This experiment was first introduced by (Chapél SubLevel Four Kenpo).

Now that we understand this mechanism, we must understand its usefulness. It is generally applicable in two situations: when we need to move our mass at high speed, or when we want to move against applied force. Its propulsion capabilities are wide ranging, I will look at the application of skips in martial technique later.

 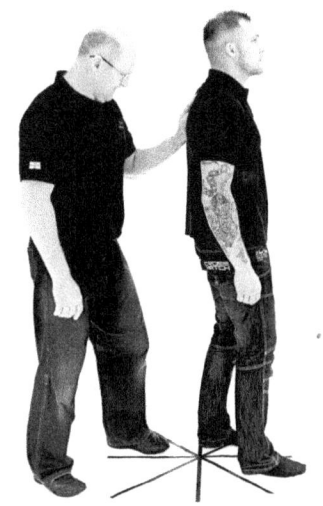

SECTION 2.6

# DIRECTIONAL HARMONY

When moving to strike or kick within the martial arts, it's important to ensure that you are moving as one unit in the same direction that you are striking in, especially when your intended outcome is power. I will be looking at power in detail later. If you are executing a strike or a kick with speed, then Directional Harmony (DH) (Parker, jr. (1992) encyclopedia of Kenpo) is not as important, as you are relying on the speed for the effectiveness of your strike. I am including DH here, as it is also a part of propulsion and will help in executing strikes and kicks more effectively. DH is self explanatory, everything has to be moving in the same direction that your weapons or blocks are, so why is it that quite often in the martial arts we step in one direction and punch in another? Is it a lack of understanding perhaps?

Here it would be helpful to take a basic move and analyse its delivery platform, so let's start with a lead jab punch. This punch is one of the most used punches around, especially in boxing. Let's go back to the neutral bow stance discussed in 1.3. Take up the neutral bow stance with your right foot forward; your right arm should be in the lead forward position. If you remain static and jab the punch out and back, the power necessary to cause damage is only as much as a person can generate from the muscles of his body. If the person executing the punch has a large muscle bulk, it will automatically be stronger than the fighter with less muscle bulk. With the right foot forward, the fighter moves his forward right foot to 9 o'clock and at the same time throws the punch out towards 12 o'clock, there is split direction of movement. Not only are body mechanics workings against you, but there is also a breakdown in the NMP. The mind is thinking that you are going sideways while you are trying to produce power forward, they are not in sync. You are propelling your body in one direction and attacking in another. This may be okay for some defensive moves, but not when you want optimum efficiency.

The following picture shows the right foot stepping to 9.00 o'clock, while the right hand is punching towards 12 o'clock (assuming that 12.00 o'clock is directly in front of you).

To create Directional Harmony Parker (1992), you have to coordinate your direction with your punch. Lift the forward foot off the ground and step forward toward your target, using your rear leg as the pushing platform. All your normal leg muscles will be engaged as you push your mass forward. As the front foot hits the floor, your jab should hit its target at the same time. Your rear foot, having propelled the body forward, needs to follow the movement of your body and not stay planted on the floor behind you. In doing so, all your mass is moving in the same direction forward. You have now created Directional Harmony.

The picture below shows stepping forward to 1 o'clock, with the right foot and punching to 12 o'clock with your right hand.

Now the majority of your mass is moving in the same direction as your punch. The above is a fairly straightforward explanation of Directional Harmony. There are many techniques that contain this theory and attention should be paid to find some of the harder techniques. One thing to remember is that if your body is moving in one direction and your strike another, you run the risk of losing power. There are exceptions to this base rule and when these exceptions are applied, we need to have other principles which come into play to gain power, but they tend not to be associated with propulsion.

SECTION 2.7

# FRONT CROSSOVER

The front crossover foot maneuver is one of the hardest and needs to be addressed. Starting in a neutral bow stance with the right foot in front, it requires you to move two full paces forward. This will require you to realign one foot and maintain the alignment of the other. We are moving forward so we need propulsion from the rear left foot. Engaging the leg muscles and pushing off while the left foot maintains its alignment as we step, creates this. At the same time that you begin to transfer your weight forward, you pivot on the ball of the right foot positioning it so that the foot points in the direction that you are moving. As your weight and mass move forward, move to the ball of the right foot and engage these muscles to support the pushing and propulsion mechanism of the body. The left foot maintains its alignment and plants while still facing 10:30. At this time, the rear right foot has reached the point where the toes are the last flexation of the foot before it leaves the ground. You will notice that the right foot is fully aligned with the whole of the leg. Ball, heel, knee and hip are all in line.

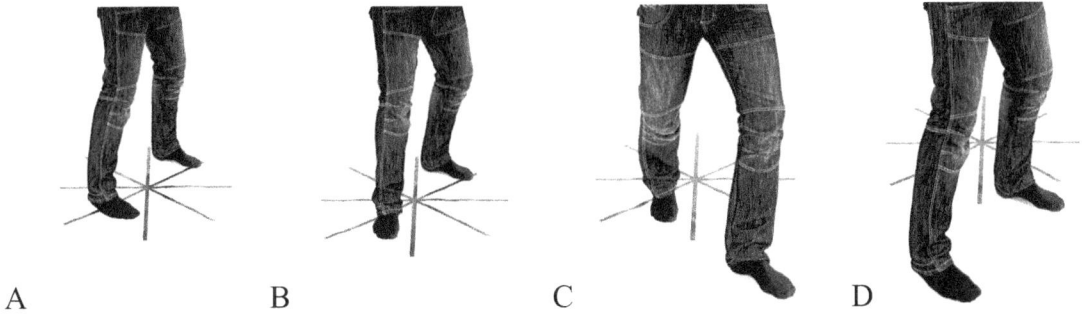

A    B    C    D

Pictures a, b, c & d, detail the required alignment of the front forward foot, ensuring that everything is facing 12 o'clock, before the transition of the rear left foot. Once the right foot leaves the ground, it changes its alignment during the swing, so that when it is again planted on the ground, it has reacquired its alignment towards 10:30. You end up in another right neutral bow stance with both feet aligned on parallel lines.

This maneuver equates to two steps forward; you have moved your mass and all body weight is moving in the forward direction. To regain your stability in the new position, the rear foot must create the PAM mechanism (Chapél (1991) course book S-101 Y). When the right foot plants lift the left foot and PAM the foot. During the execution of this maneuver, we establish what is called a transitional stance midway between the movements. If you stop at this point, you will have created a front twist stance with a very well aligned rear foot. There are many transitional stances found within foot maneuvers and the above explanation will help the reader identify more of these.

# 3 ASYMMETRICAL MOVEMENT AND SPEED

This chapter is about simple body mechanics of the human body, how the body seeks symmetry, and how asymmetry helps our bodies move with speed, efficiency and power. We'll see how this is incorporated and taught within martial arts. We'll also learn a few more of the principles and theories to help us understand biomechanical movement and some of the reasons behind the movements we perform.

SECTION 3.1

# BODY SYMMETRY

What do I mean when I talk about the symmetry that the human body seeks? And yes, it does seek symmetry. In most cases we do it naturally without having to consciously think about it. Only when we take it out of this subconscious thought process and apply it to conscious thought are we able to make extraordinary improvements in the way we move. Symmetry has a direct effect on speed, power, alignment principles, and many more areas within the martial arts, here I will take a couple of principles and expand on them. Once you have taken the improvements on board, it is then time to engrain them into your muscle pathways, working towards being able to assign them back to your subconscious. Then you will access them without conscious thought, and your speed and power will increase experientially. For this process to work at its best, we need to be able to really understand what is happening, why we do certain movements, and what does not work.

Let's look at a simple example of what I mean when I say the body seeks symmetry. Take an Olympic sprinter as an example. Mentally picture the last time you observed the athlete in full flight. What does his body mechanics teach us? The first thing that should strike you is how the upper body helps drive the legs. When the right leg is powering forward, the left arm is doing the same movement, and it's a reverse of what's happening on the ground. When the left leg is finishing its stride behind, the right arm is doing the same. Everything works in harmony to power the body forward. All these mechanics come together subconsciously, if the athlete were to think about each action, they would lose coordination, speed and power. Imagine tying the right arm of the race winner to his side and then repeat the race. He won't be able to work at his optimum; his body will be out of sync and it will not work symmetrically. He is not capable of obtaining the same high level of performance because his movement is unnatural. Now let's take a martial application of movement and see how an understanding of symmetry can improve strikes or blocks. One of the actions I teach is something that is called a Slap check (Chapél (1991) course 101 Y). This has several applications, what I want to do here is cover its relationship to symmetry, speed and power.

Experiment 4:

1, Raise your right arm up to a horizontal plane with your fist no higher than your shoulder. Imagine a symmetrical box, which is formed from left shoulder to your right shoulder, out in front of your right shoulder, across in front of you then back to your left shoulder. Make sure that your fist does not change its position from its natural alignment.

A                                B                                C

Picture A, shows the right arm positioned, before execution of the backfist and then returning to its original starting position picture C. Have the fist slightly out in front of the box, so that your arm has formed an obtuse angle. Have your left hand open and positioned facing forward at the same height as your left shoulder.

2, With your right hand, execute a back fist strike as fast as you can, striking a target that is in line with your right shoulder at the end of your reach with your arm. Do not over extend or lean. Execute this with your left hand still.

3, Once this has been done attempt to execute the same strike, but this time move your left hand to your right shoulder slowly. This movement is what we call a slap check; when the left hand touches the shoulder ensure that the hand is high enough so that the fingers slightly overlap the shoulder. What you will find here is that it is almost impossible for you to carry out the prescribed movement in this way. You simply cannot move one arm fast and the other slow.

4. The last part of this experiment is to execute both movements as fast as you can. What can help here is not to think about the right hand, but think about the left moving as fast as it can from its starting position to your right shoulder and back to its original position. Do the same thing with your right arm, from its point of origin out to its target and back again. Thinking one move in front of another is what we call perception speed; you think your moves fast!

Performing the movement as described in section 2. 4 above increases your speed significantly. If your intention is to execute a speed strike, it should be just that fast. It does not have to have any power principles to back it up; its effectiveness relies on speed. The quicker it moves, the more velocity it has, resulting in more damage caused. Without the body moving symmetrically, you will not be able to move it at your highest velocity and in your most effective manner. When you are launching a weapon away from its platform at high speed, the action required to stop your fist mentally is hard. Damage can occur at this point as your muscles work to halt your arm traveling at high speed. That's why it needs a target to hit and dissipate its energy into. The hit is the trigger telling the brain to stop the strike and begin its returning motion. When you move both hands at the same speed, the slap check hitting the shoulder is the corresponding trigger to stop the left hand. Everything works symmetrically.

One of the easiest movements to see symmetry in motion within the martial arts is the traditional reverse punch: as one hand is hitting, the other is returning. If power is required, the returning arm has to return with power. The key is to understand this movement, to know how and what you are trying to achieve, and practice it repeatedly so that it will be put back into your subconscious. When this happens, it will become even faster, as you no longer have to rely on conscious thought. You will have Neuromuscular Body Programming built in. Conscious thought, or cognitive thought, is in itself slower than your subconscious thought process. To create action takes 0.2 of a second from your thought to your action; to react to action takes 0.5 of a second.

With any movement, it is important to remember that extra little adjustments here and there will ultimately slow you down. The trick is to keep it simple and keep your body aligned. If you do this, your body will instinctively know what it's trying to achieve and it will help you to your goal. The body is a fascinating machine capable of highly efficient movement; we just forget how to harness this ability when teaching or moving in any martial art. Of course, the opposite is also true. We have the ability to learn to move in ways that are not always as efficient as they could be.

SECTION 3.2

# STARTLE REFLEX

Another point to consider here is the speed in which the body can react to different stimuli, for example, the startle reflex. If we look at the speed the body is capable of moving at while this reflex is occurring, you may notice that it is exceptionally fast and not reliant upon body symmetry. Imagine putting your hand out to turn the handle of a door that has been superheated. Once the stimulus receptors registered the danger, your hand will disengage the handle at lightning speed. It is not dependent on the other hand moving at the same speed, since it is protecting itself and is not within the mechanics of normal movement. The startle reflex has been associated with the surprise emotion, so, is it a reflex or is it an emotion? One thing is for sure; it's a non-cognitive move. If we have to think about it, it's already too late. The emotion of surprise is a reaction due to a thought process, and at this point it differs from a startle. Emotions are the body's way of telling the outside world what's going on within the person, such as fear, surprise, sadness, etc. The startle reflex is an inbuilt innate protection mechanism.

The only way that we have a chance of moving at such a high speed consciously is to ensure that we are moving as efficiently and naturally as possible. If our movement is anything else, then we run the risk of being too slow, yet speed is not always the desired outcome. There may well be times when speed is redundant to power. This will depend upon the circumstances. However, power cannot occur without the input of speed. The creation of a startle usually comes from one of the three senses: sight, sound, and touch, with the first two being the major causes of a startle. Our eyes pick up any movement towards the face and reflex, depending upon the threat perceived. It can be as simple as a blink. Our hearing does the same, usually causing the body to reflex when a very loud and unexpected noise occurs.

In the martial arts, having an understanding of the startle reflex can be beneficial, it can make the difference between doing a move because you are told to and understanding that you do a move in a particular way because you are trying to make a startle reflex happen, to make your attacker move. If we observe a beginner in the martial arts and have someone throw a punch towards the head, the first thing that we see is the movement of the head away from the incoming danger. No sophisticated block, just a very simple movement of the head. They are reacting to the threat without any training. If the punch comes straight at them, they will normally react by moving the head backwards first, followed by the body in the same direction. A wave occurs throughout the body and can go as far as the knees bending and the person then putting their hands out to protect the body from hitting the ground.

A very simple application of this reaction would be the intended result from a feint punch. You are not really intending the feint to hit, just to cause some level of reaction. We use this move to momentarily distract our attacker while we move to our planned major attack. A finger poke to the eyes is one of the most effective techniques within the martial arts. It does not take an eighteen stone muscle-bound guy to perform this technique; in fact, if a four stone child performs this move, it has a profound effect on the eighteen stone guy, as the eyes are the weakest targets on the human body. The interesting question here is can the eye poke be performed at the same level of violence as a punch?

The body has the capability to move at very fast speeds, often so fast that the eyes have difficulty in following the movement, so if you are going to strike toward or into the eyes, be prepared for a fast startle reaction. Any strike into the eyes will create pain due to the sensory input that the eyes are capable of taking in. Any strike toward or into the eyes will initially create a startle reflex, while pain will be a secondary response. As with most reactions affecting the body, there is the initial reaction followed by responses due to shock. This is known as the fight or flight response. There is a distinct difference between the body's reaction to pain and a startle reflex.

This difference lies within how the human nervous system works. With the startle reflex, the neurons produced by the body entering the startle reflex never reach the brain. Instead, they enter a region of our upper spinal column known as the spinal reflex centre. From here a loop is created and the body part sending the message moves in a reflex manner, when firing electrochemical transmitters return to the transmitting body part. When the body moves fast to a pain stimulus, it has to first register pain in our brain and then sends the message to the body part to move.

Hence this type of movement is innately slower than the startle reflex. The most common reaction to a startle reflex is that the major extremities, including the head, retract to the core of our body. This means that the head moves in a very similar fashion as a turtles head, retracting into its shell for protection. Your chin and head drop along with the rising of the shoulders. The arms move backwards and usually towards the centre of the chest. The legs also retract, bending at the knees and the hips and folding into the core. This posture is much like the fetal posture taken when we curl the body up.

Throughout this type of reaction, it's important to remember that the limbs are traveling at their quickest speed. All the prime mover muscles will have been turned off, with the limbs moving using fast twitch muscles only. These are the muscle groups that allow our body to move itself at speed. This is an extremely important biomechanical movement, especially in relation to moving within the martial arts, if we want to move as fast as we can.

SECTION 3.3

# TIMING

When striking in the martial arts, we often have certain moves or sequences designed to improve our timing, which are not always apparent to the beginner. Timing is one of those actions that can be attributed to skill. If someone moves well, they often move with good timing and coordination, but how do we analyse timing?

The first thing to consider is how do we discern what timing is. If we are practicing a combination of moves which requires us to move quickly, what you will find is that most students, when they first learn a set of movements, follow each move with their eyes, trying to think what's the next move and the next and the next, resulting in constipated movement. Although we have to first work with the eyes to understand where each move has to go, once this has been engrained, the best way to increase speed and timing is to listen to the beat of the moves.

Our hearing plays an important role in creating speed of movement. Without going into music in depth, let's look at how beats are applied to the martial arts. As with dance, once we have timing, rhythm and coordination, we are well on the way to moving well. The beats that apply here are full beat, half beat, quarter beat, and syncopated. A full beat is defined in music as 4/4 or 1, 2, 3, 4, 1, 2, 3, 4 and so on. The time between the beat is extenuated but not too long, In the martial arts this is seen when a student stands in a training stance and executes a straight punch while the instructor counts the numbers to the beat. The student finds it relatively easy to keep in time and coordinate with others.

The half and quarter beat are quicker repetition of beats. What we need to look at is how knowing and listening to these beats can help as we move. If we can move our body and our strikes in time with half and quarter beats, we can increase the speed of our movement. If you are in a combat situation and just moved at a full beat pace, your movement would soon become predictable, which is something to avoid. Quite often when students begin to move and perform a set technique on their opponent, they move in a set rhythm, moving from one move to another then to another and become trapped in the movement of their body. The rhythm they move in when in this state of action is a continuous beat. It may be a quick full beat, but it is still a full beat with no pauses within the motion. Within any fighting situation, you must be able to perceive, adapt and change, and this will only happen if your timing is not continuous. Let's look at broken rhythm and timing signatures. Broken rhythm (Parker, jr, (1992) encyclopedia of Kenpo) is a point within any set of moves where you pause or change the timing of your strikes or movement. The reason to break your own rhythm is that you will never be able to have a cast iron guarantee that the person will react in exactly the way that you think they will. You may find that your first move is so good and their reaction is so violent that they are no longer within your range. Any pre-planned move you have after that simply will not work. If you were locked into the mindset and beat of the moves without understanding broken rhythm, you would be wasting strikes, executing them into thin air. It is no good to have great speed with no ability to change or alter that speed. You not only have your own rhythm to consider, but you also have the rhythm of your attacker. They have their own rhythm that is often linked to their planned attack.

If you are an attacker and your plan is to hit the person in front of you with two punches, a straight left jab followed by a right cross or roundhouse punch, and the person is just standing there and giving you no outward sign that he is trained, then in your mind you have a plan: 1 2. That's your timing signature and your rhythm is how quickly you do each punch. Pre-planned techniques all have their own timing signatures. This is where moves can be preset, and then you pause and move on. The difference between a signature and broken rhythm is that the signature happens no matter what the reaction, as reactions are predictable within certain parameters. We can increase our beats to quarter beats to ensure that a strike is landed before the attacker is out of range. This all relates to the speed and movement of our body when forced with a fight situation.

That leaves us with syncopated beats. The simplest way to understand this is to try to imagine striking with two limbs at the same time. If you take the example in 3.1 when I described the action of a back fist, the fist and the hand are on first examination hitting together. This is not the most effective timing. What we want to achieve is the open hand touching our shoulder a split second in front of the back fist hitting its target; this way the result will be an increase in the penetration and power of your strike, the timing is syncopated. If you hold two balls of exactly the same weight above the ground, with one 10 mm higher than the other, then let them go together, one would hit the ground a fraction sooner before the other. Yet it is very difficult to perceive which one hits the floor first as they are so close together.

The following pictures show two balls held at different heights, being dropped and landing with syncopated timing.

SECTION 3.4

# METHODS OF DELIVERY

There is a limited amount of ways in which any block or strike can be delivered. The main difference is thrusting and snapping. The thrust action is slower than the snap, and its primary aim is to produce power, although speed of delivery is important. This is in direct contrast to a snapping action, where the technique will be more effective if high speed can be achieved. The higher the speed generated, the greater the effect of the weapon on the target. Speed consists of several components. The equation of speed is, "The rate of position change with time." We've seen the need for the body to move asymmetrically to enable it to work in its most efficient fastest manner. Yet there are other principles to look at concerning speed. They are velocity, acceleration recoil, and mechanics. Velocity is speed with direction, from point A to point B, the greater the velocity, the greater the impact. To get to a high rate of speed, you must accelerate the limb in question from standstill to high speed. Acceleration is the change in velocity over time. It is very important that you build up your speed over time. You must ensure that the muscles of the limbs are trained to understand the movement being required of them. If you try to move in a way that your body is not used to, it is very easy to pull muscles or strain tendons. The fact that a fast strike relies on speed to cause damage means that the higher the velocity from its point of origin to the target, the greater the damage. If you use your fist and strike a hard target at speed, damage will occur, both to the target and your hand.

To create velocity through the body, the correct path of action and biomechanical sequencing needs to be employed with any strike, with each sequential move drawing speed from each other, so that the end velocity of the backfist for example, is determined from all that goes before it. If stepping forward and executing a backfist, the end velocity is gained from the speed and velocity of each sequential move that is behind the one technique. The step through, pelvic movement, and torso rotation all help in gearing up the velocity of the final move.

Take a step through front snapping kick as another example. From a left fighting stance, move through the sequences discussed in 2.2. The kicking leg moves from its rear position and swings through underneath the hip, taking speed from the thigh as its moves forward of the hip to initiate the kick. In the power stage of this move, the whole leg moves quickly to bring the thigh and the knee into position to launch the kicking foot. The velocity built up through this power stage is transferred to the lower leg, which then snaps forward with even greater velocity. The foot at this time is traveling very fast, so it is important to ensure that damage does not happen. On impact there is recoil, just like when the firing pin of a gun strikes the bullet and the gun jumps away from the impact.

The pictures below show the effects of firing a gun and the resulting recoil.

Recoil should be used to your advantage. Starting your reverse motion and following the asymmetrical rule, return to your point of origin. Use the recoil to trigger this movement, as it is a natural occurrence of impact. The other natural occurrence is the dissipation of energy into the target, with an opposite amount of energy being transferred back from the target into your body. This will be absorbed through your limbs, body and ultimately the ground. Since we are made of 78- 82% water, this energy is seldom felt at a cognitive level.

The following pictures show the right leg lifted up creating a 90% angle between the horizontal upper leg and the lower leg. This is where the hinge occurs when the kick is executed.

To facilitate the execution of speed, make sure the limb and weapon being employed are used in line with your natural body movement. When executing strikes by the hand or the foot, try to maintain your hinge joint (knee cap to foot) in a stable position and move the lower limb around this joint. This type of movement around a joint is known as angular movement. If executed correctly, you can build a tremendous amount of speed. If you set your whole arm moving and then snap the lower limb around the elbow, even more speed will be created. The problem with this is the elbow is extended while the arm is moving, making it very hard to apply the brakes. Also in this type of movement, hyperextension of the elbow is a very distinct possibility. The biomechanical term for this is hyper adduction. The two prime movements of muscles needed to produce speed of movement are flexion and extension. The type of muscle will also have a direct effect on speed. There are some muscles that simply cannot work at high speed as they are made of slow twitch fibers. To enable our bodies to move at speed, we need to ensure that the muscle groups used have a high degree of fast twitch fibers. These will then aid us with moving at our fastest velocity possible.

Whipping - We are all familiar with the crack of a whip and how the noise generated is created: the tip of the whip travels faster than sound and so causes the crack. It is possible to deliver strikes in this manner. This method of execution is advanced and should be trained over a long period of time, as damage is possible. The whip can be defined as a wave that transfers energy through it and comes to a point upon impact. To create this method of delivery takes a great deal of skill, coordination, and understanding of body mechanics. The end result can be devastating if executed properly. One of the major differences with this type of delivery is the lack of stability required. The body has to be in a constant state of fluid imbalance; it has to be buoyant throughout the entire execution.

The technique description below will use the backfist discussed in 3.1. With so many martial art techniques, the whip starts from the feet and contact with the ground.

From a right fighting stance, load your weight onto your rear left foot by bending your knee. As you straighten this leg, transfer the wave movement from your rear foot through your knee into your left hip. The wave continues through your right hip and up through your main trunk. A twist needs to occur as you move the wave into the right shoulder. At the same time you need to load your left shoulder by moving it forward, and as your left shoulder is returning on its wave pattern, this releases the right shoulder. The right shoulder needs to push your right elbow forward and as your right elbow extends, your right fist comes back towards you and then gets whipped to the full extension of your arm at the very last instant toward the target. This all has to be executed while buoyant and fluid, with your absolute focus concentrated on the last flex with the fist. If required, the hand could also open and the fingertips used as the last weapon.

## SECTION 3.5

# PSYCHOLOGICAL SPEED

The first determining part of any movement is the central nervous system, which is made up of the brain and the spinal cord; from these all human movement is initiated, controlled and monitored. The next step in controlling movement is the peripheral nervous system, which constitutes every nerve outside of the central nervous system. This system in itself has several subsystems; the one that I am concerned with here is the autonomic nervous system.

This system is the one humans use every second of every day of their lives and without any cognitive thought. It controls functions such as heartbeat, breathing, and initiates many of our reflexes. It is used when we walk, run, drive, swim and many other normal everyday activities. This is also the one system that it takes an effort to become aware of. The control of this system and the movement undertaken by it can be categorised as spontaneous actions. When we use our minds to interact with this system, introducing a conscious thought process, the moves produced by this interaction are faster than any other conscious movement, as they are imbedded in the subconscious mind and controlled by the autonomic nervous system.

Can you recall a time when a stressful situation occurred and time seemed to slow down? Your mind is working so fast that you are able to think many moves in front of the next. This is the same type of experience that I am exploring here. The body and mind can be trained with certain moves in such a way that speed of movement is increased. The key here is the ability to take a specific movement out of your subconscious, put it into your conscious mind, analyse it, practice it slowly, and then over time put the move back into your subconscious, so that it becomes spontaneous.

I believe that the highest skill level of any martial artist, regardless of style, should be moving spontaneously. This is where the essence of true psychological speed exists. Assume that you find yourself in a position where you are able to hammer fist strike an attacker's groin. Your next move from the hammer fist is a rising elbow to underneath their jaw. The first consideration here is the reaction of your attacker after the hit. Assume that your strike is perfect and it has caught them in the ideal spot and they are now entering a reflex action.

The pictures below show the reaction at different stages of a strike to the groin.

If we study the action caused by a strike to the groin in this manner, what we will find is that the body does not travel backwards; also the hips are not forced backwards. What happens when a true reflex occurs to this stimulus? The body collapses upon itself, the knees give way, and depending upon the amount of force, the body will drop to the ground.

The following pictures show three different stages of the reaction to a hammer fist to the groin, the head meets the rising elbow.

The initial strike and your attacker's reaction are what are known as the ideal phase; everything is working perfectly. Your next planned move is the rising elbow. It's simple to believe that this can be executed without any problem. However, this is not the case if your attacker has innately entered a reflex to pain. They will be moving spontaneously and at a very high speed. Your next planned move has to be equal to or faster than the attacker's reflex action. At this point psychological speed can be employed. You have to know your next move, your attackers reaction to the move and already be thinking ahead of it. This is done by focusing not on the elbow rising or on the elbow returning down from the strike, but on the position of the hand before the move has even began. The point of origin of the elbow is the position it has reached after the strike to the groin. The elbow needs to move up and then down, returning to its original point of origin in a split second.

If you can train this thought process into the move, you will be able to move at a lightning speed, which is just as fast as your attacker's pain reflex. As the elbow is lower than the jaw, they will meet and collide quickly. This type of collision is called an initiated collision (Chapél (1991) course 101 Y). You are causing the attacker to move in such a way that they collide with your strike. The real key here is that you understand how speed is developed. By inserting into the above move a symmetrical movement with the other moving limb, just imagine the speed in which you can move.

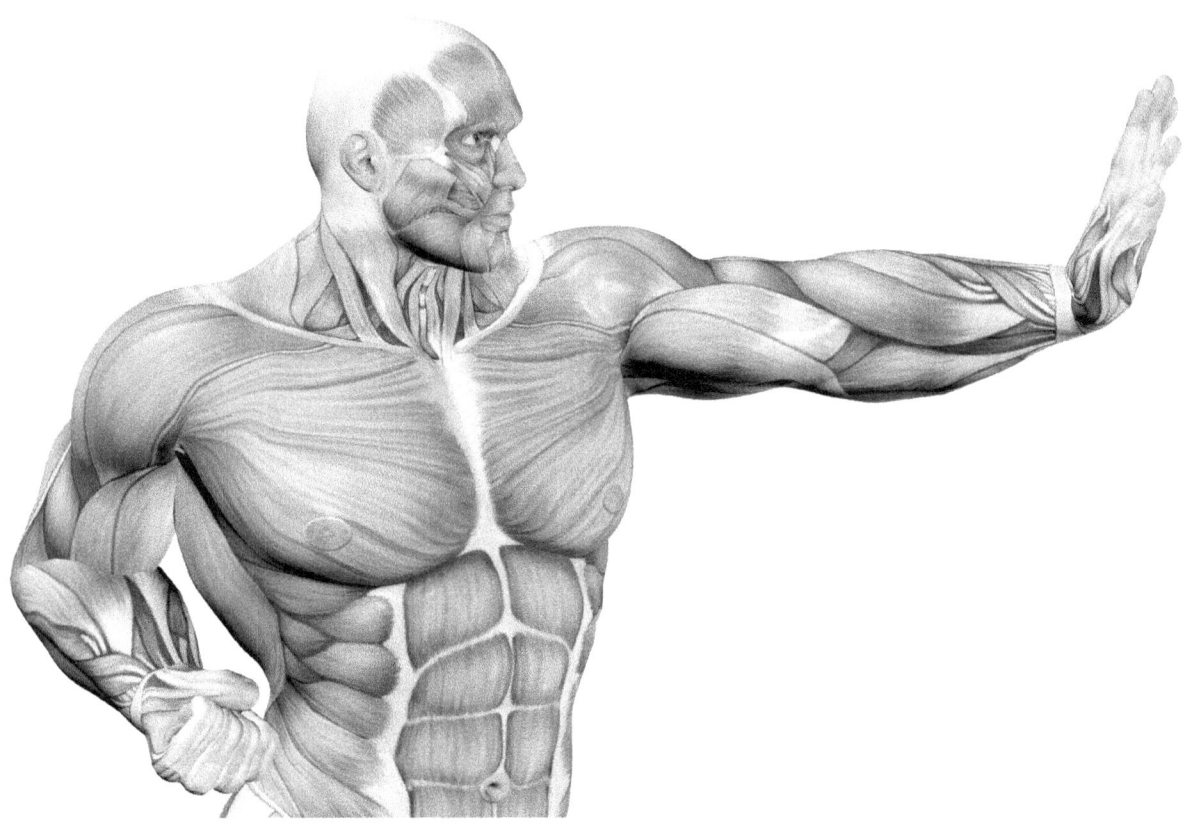

# 4 POWER PRINCIPLES OF STRIKES

This chapter will explore the theory and principles of producing power with the human body. The generation of power is a key aim within the martial arts, the theories and principles will help any art or individual understand how this is achieved and will enable them to enhance their power.

SECTION 4.1

# THE BASICS

The basics of power are often overlooked. Instructors sometimes teach through the words, "Keep practicing that way and power will come." This chapter is about how that power comes, or more accurately, how we can understand the body mechanics necessary to produce effective and efficient power.

Power is defined as Mass x Speed = Power. Transfer that equation to the human body and what do you get? Total confusion! Power is the body's ability to channel strength, to transfer force through the body into a strike or block. If executed well, power will result and the effects of this power will be obvious to the observer and be felt by your attacker. If you watch someone execute a strike, you will often notice a recoiling of the attacking weapon at the last second. I refer to this as pulling. This trained action can easily be overcome by practicing your strikes on a punch bag. This will give you the necessary experience of striking an object without the recoil, you will also feel resistance. All of this is very important when practicing the martial arts. If you insert the recoil into the above equation, what is the result? Mass x Speed – Recoil (pulling) = no power generation going forward at the point of impact.

To practice executing power, it must be done in such a manner as not to create badly learned behavior. You must delete the recoil/pulling from the equation and insert accuracy and control to ensure that any moves will be effective, on target, and safe. To generate power moving in a direction, you must engage your mass and move it forward. This links to Directional Harmony, i.e. all of your body moving in the direction of the attack, producing inertia, and moving it in an aligned manner rather than being misaligned. To help us analyse the above I will use a particular technique, this way we can understand how efficient and effective the principles under discussion are. If you use all the above and add speed, then you have power. There are three major principles to help us understand and produce power: backup mass, rotational torque, and gravitational force (Parker (1987) vol. 5). Which one comes first? To have any power at all in a martial application, you need to move the mass, so it stands to reason that backup mass is first. For example, take a reverse punch, executed from a left fighting stance. This makes the right fist the weapon of choice and the attacker's right rib cage the intended target, assuming that the attacker steps towards you and throws a right punch toward your head. This technique is the pinnacle of power within the martial arts. Now look at the technique in a stationary mode. The neutral bow stance is taken up to give you some control over your width. Width is defined as the amount of your body exposed to your attacker. By bringing your width into play, you rotate around the left hip, which is helped by pushing your right foot out. This means the right foot is now facing 12 o'clock. This action is your rotational torque element for producing power. This in turn brings the right shoulder forward and allows you to release your right fist for the reverse punch.

The pictures below show the body during the stages of a reverse punch.

Now we need to analyse this movement further if we are to really understand what we are doing mechanically and what we are trying to achieve with the body. Single hip and double hip rotation can also be used to enhance the production of power through the hips. This will be covered in future writings.

SECTION 4.2

# BACK UP MASS

To understand this principle, take a normal size family car traveling at fifty mph. On impact with a wall there will be a certain amount of damage. Now take an 18-wheel lorry, traveling at the same speed and hitting the same wall: the damaged caused will be far greater. Why? Mass x Speed = Power, so the larger the mass or weight behind the strike, the greater the power.

Producing backup mass with the body is not quite so simple. You just can't run fast at someone and create power with a strike, there is a little more to it than that. The whole body has to be behind the strike and moving in the same direction. If you step to the side and punch straight ahead, you will not have 100% of your mass behind your weapon.

Earlier I discussed the reverse punch from a stable and static position. To bring effectiveness into this strike and to use backup mass efficiently, you need to move. At the same time that you move your mass, you also need to synchronise the other power principles, but for now let's just look at how you can move. The maneuver required to bring backup mass into this technique is a step drag. From a left fighting stance, lift the forward foot clear off the ground and step forward, maintaining correct foot alignment with the forward foot facing 1:30. The distance taken with the first step will be dependent upon the fighting gap and how far you need to move to bring your mass into play. You cannot take a deep long step, as this will extend the depth of your stance well beyond your natural ability to bring your rear foot with you. You will become planted to the floor as your weight drops on impact of your forward foot to the floor, so the distance is critical. For clarity's sake, set the distance at the width of your own foot. If this is 200mm, then the step will be 200mm. Now that the forward left foot has moved, move the rear right foot.

The movement of the left foot is created by spring loading your rear leg to allow you to lift the forward foot and propel it forward. The straightening of the rear leg is the launching platform As your mass is propelled forward, this allows you to lift the rear foot and bring it with you, rotating the right hip around the left hip as we move the rear foot. On planting the rear foot, the foot should face 12 o'clock and the direction you are moving.

The following pictures show the detail of the foot, with the ball of the foot hitting the ground first, followed by the heel.

Plant the ball of the foot first, then flex the foot and plant the heel down a moment later. When this happens, the rear leg straightens, transferring momentum from the rear foot, through the leg and into the hip. It's at this point that the torso has to rotate in line with the hips, which also brings your right shoulder around at the same time, creating the launching platform for the punch. What this sequencing has done is bring together the biomechanical movement of the body to produce backup mass, or your whole body propelling forward to bring power to your punch. This comes together on impact of the punch and needs to be aligned in such a way that the mass is fully behind your fist.

SECTION 4.3

# INERTIA

Inertia is a Law of Motion, the first of three laws of motion introduced by Sir Isaac Newton. This Law states that every body continues in a state of rest or of uniform motion in a straight line, unless it is compelled to change that state by forces applied to it.

Inertia is directly linked to mass. There are forces within the body that create a change in the state of our own mass, i.e. we can alter our direction when moving, or initiate movement. We do not need an external stimulus to affect our state. We are not like an object continually in a state of zero velocity until an external force is applied, nor an object moving in a direction that would continue to do so until its direction is altered by another force. The greater the mass, the greater the inertia created. This is counterbalanced by the size of the muscles controlling the mass, meaning that the larger the mass, the greater the force behind a strike. We can choose to become buoyant and move in just about any direction that we want; it's a matter of which movement is desired and whether it is effective in a martial application.

The step drag is an example of choosing to initiate forward momentum and by doing so create inertia. We can continue this movement forward and increase the rate of velocity and the amount of inertia that comes with increased speed. We also have the choice to stabilise our mass at any given moment to help increase the effectiveness of our action. The aim of the step drag is to move mass and create inertia, putting backup mass behind the punch at the point of contact, plus having everything that the floor has to offer in the form of stability to aid our power.

Remember: all that is being analysed here are power principles applied to the body. Inertia can be affected within the body by control over the muscle structure.

Experiment 5:

1. Walking at a steady pace in a straight line, suddenly stop. You will have to plant whichever foot is moving forward with enough commitment to stop your forward momentum.

2. Increase your walk to a steady jog and repeat the above.

3. Run at a fast pace and repeat the stopping exercise with care.

In 1, it is relatively easy to stop the forward momentum of the body. The lower platform will stop quickly, though the upper mass above the hips will want to continue forward, your head being the last proportion to bring under control. The natural inertia created by your walk will suddenly stop and your own inertia will then come through the foot up into your forward knee, acting much like a shock absorber, bending to absorb the mass and inertia of your upper body. In 2 and 3, you will not be able to stop in one step. The legs will take up the force and inertia, but you will not be able to simply stop. If you could, your upper mass and inertia would continue and you would fall forward to the ground. The faster you are moving at the point when you initiate the stop, the harder it is for you to bring your own inertia under control. It can be done over time; it's just not instant. You control your own movement and you have control to a degree over the Law of Inertia. It all depends upon your choice of movement.

SECTION 4.4

# **ROTATIONAL TORQUE**

Rotational torque (Parker, (1987) vol. 4) in the above reverse punch technique power occurs when the right hip torques around the left hip while you move your right foot into position. To create and understand torque within body movement requires a base understanding of how torque occurs.

Torque from your biomechanical movement is force acting a distance away from the axis of rotation. Within the hip movement above, the axis of rotation is on the vertical plane, with the axis running down through the left hip. As the right hip is being rotated around this axis, power is increased in the movement of the right hip and the right side of the body. The next stage of rotational torque is created through the execution of the right punch. It does not really matter where the punch is coming from; wherever it is, that is the right fist's point of origin for this particular technique, i.e. held on the right hip or positioned in guard. For the sake of clarity, position the fist in the traditional position, with the fist already formed and high on the right side.

The pictures below show various stages of a reverse punch, during execution torque occurs.

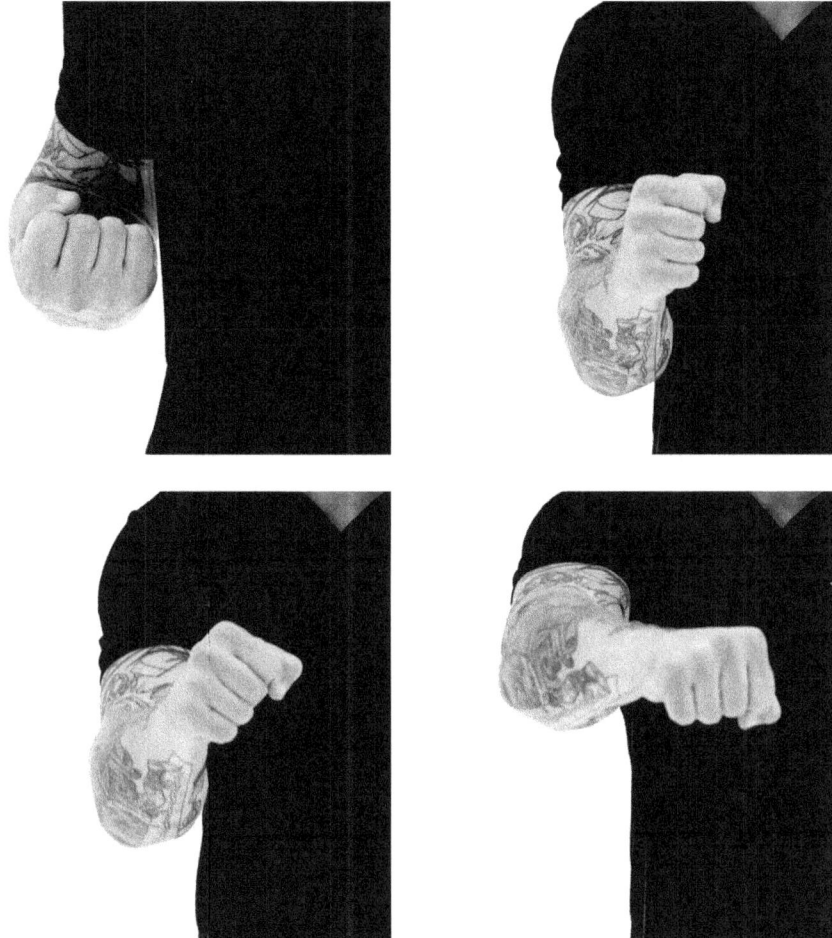

As you begin to launch the fist towards its target, the hand must stay positioned with the palm facing upward while the arm is extended.

There are several different delivery methods, but for the ease of understanding, I have chosen a basic move that many martial arts teach. Just before impact, the fist rotates through a horizontal axis and force is generated around the axis and focused into the fist. There are two major considerations to be made at this point.

1 The cause and effect of this rotation, when the collision occurs on the target.

2 The biomechanical use of Functional Anatomy.

It is difficult to set up an experiment looking at the effects of a certain collision on the human body, as this would mean being hit and hit reasonably hard. For the sake of safety, let's look at two different applications of a collision caused by a punch that is being executed as described above. I have already defined the rotational execution, the second method is to have the fist already positioned at the waist, as it would be upon impact, in other words, no torque dynamics, just the use of the arm and the fist. This type of execution would benefit from the same dynamics and principles discussed earlier, when executing this punch, the only difference being torque. The angle of incidence (Parker, jr. (1992) encyclopedia of Kenpo) of the punch on the attacker's body will be the same for both methods of delivery, hitting at 90 degrees to the target.

The collision in the second application without torque mechanics will be more like a blunt thrust directly into the body of your attacker. A collision will occur and force will be transferred from your whole movement, through your body, down your arm, through your fist, and into your attacker's body. The pictures below show a fist hitting the body at an angle of 90 and 45 degrees. Torque will generate a different type of impact, as it will contain rotation.

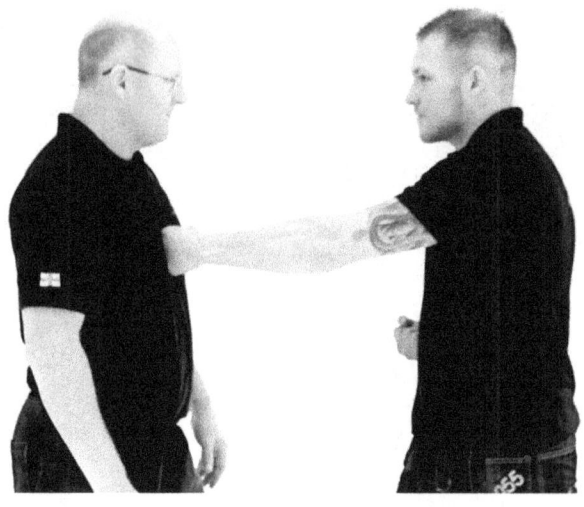

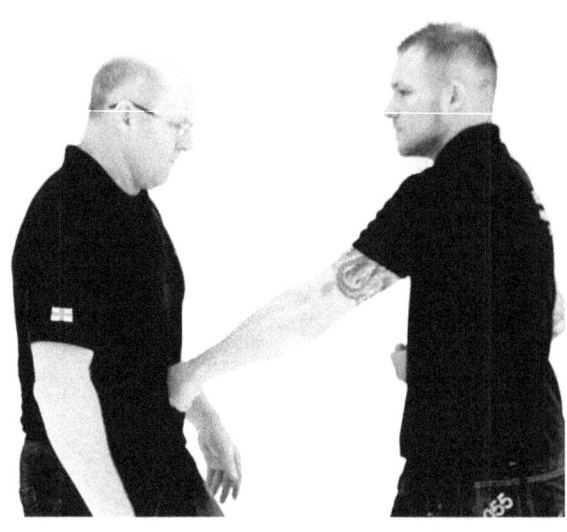

The picture below shows a punching arm fully extended.

To discuss joint and arm positions, we must first define the angle of the arm. At this point the two bones within your forearm, the ulna and the radius, have rotated and twist around each other. Angles are created when there are two relative segments, and in this case it's the upper arm and the forearm. In the final position, the arm and forearm are fully extended, so there is no angle between them. For efficient use of the arm within the mechanics of a punch, to overextend it to point 180 (locked out) is detrimental to the effectiveness of the punch and penetration. Over time, the arm will be damaged by this hyper adduction to point 180. If instead of the over extension defined above you train to stop the arm before the 180-point, you will always have force left in your muscles to transfer into the attacker.

Look at the position of the final punch to ensure that an angle of 170 degrees is maintained between the upper arm and the forearm. The position of the fist from a frontal view shows that the fist still has rotation to go before lockout happens.

The picture below shows the right punching arm extended, with a slight bend at the elbow. The frontal view of the fist creates a diamond shape.

## SECTION 4.5

# GRAVITATIONAL FORCE

One of the less obvious applications of power is that of gravity. In the example of the reverse punch it is difficult to see it at first, but if at the point of impact you can settle your mass, then you increase the effect of the strike and the power produced.

Newton termed the law of force acting upon objects falling to the ground as gravity. An object, when accelerating from zero velocity to the ground, creates a force. From the moment we begin to stand and walk on our feet, we are constantly subjected to the force of gravity. The structure used to counteract this force is the skeletal frame supported by the muscles of the body. Every muscle works in some way to maintain the structure, to move the body, and ultimately counter the force of gravity. The amount of gravitational force (Parker (1987) vol4) generated through the body is directly linked to the weight or mass we bring to bear and the greater the mass, the greater the force that can be delivered.

If you fall on another person, power is generated. Using this force to increase the power and effectiveness of any strike is not an easy one. It takes practice to disengage the muscles that support the body just before the moment of impact and then re-engage them to maintain posture. Another really important point here is that the strike being executed has to travel downward. Delivering a strike on the horizontal or vertical plane receives no benefit from the use of gravity. it all has to combine at the point of impact. The technique of a reverse punch can be used again as an example. The most important aspect of the position of the arm, which is delivering the punch, is that it will have to be angled downward. Viewing the body position from the side in the picture below, you can see the importance of the angle.

When at the point of impact you drop your weight, force is transferred into another person. From the three basic principles of power inertia, rotational torque, and gravitational force we have the base principles necessary to produce power within the human body and transfer this to another individual. The effectiveness of any strike depends upon these principles, as well as timing, acceleration, coordination, focus, mindset, NMP, Directional Harmony, and a host of other skills; this is what effective striking is all about.

SECTION 4.6

# BODY ALIGNMENT

There are other alignment angles to consider in techniques and a term to illustrate my point is a "Braced Angle." (Parker, jr, (1992) encyclopedia of Kenpo). If the whole body is aligned in the correct manner at the point of impact as discussed, you will have the benefit of this angle to help brace the body against the force of the impact transferred back into your body.

This picture shows the body in a reverse punch position arm angled down, this indicates the alignment all the way through the body from the end of the fist to the ground.

The angle created with your body is braced from the floor all the way up through the leg, hip, torso, shoulder, and finally into the hand on the right side of your body. To have dimensionally accurate angles within the body, the left side also has to support the right side, it is necessary to create this for the overall brace, and good posture must be maintained. Blocking is another aspect that requires correct body alignment. The angles that may be achieved with the arms when blocking have to support and absorb force. If your blocks are not correctly aligned their effect will be compromised. Body alignment and posture go hand in hand together, if your alignment is out, this will have a direct effect on your posture. Over time bad posture will have a negative effect on the body and its ability to move and maintain itself structurally. Undue forces will be applied throughout the skeletal frame, the result of which will be evidenced by joints breaking down, excess deposits of fat being overlaid at problem areas and general aches and pains. Misaligned joints can affect the whole health of the body. The applied application of misaligned joints and limbs within a martial application will very quickly be discovered, when injuries start to happen.

SECTION 4.7

# PSYCHOLOGY OF POWER

Not only are the correct biomechanical movements needed, and the coming together of all the above principles necessary to achieve power, but also a correct mindset is crucial. If not, all the above is nothing but talk. Part of this is the thought process behind the pulling of the punch. When a punch is practiced in this way, it is usually for a reason; in this case, the protection of your partner. In pulling the punch and using the thought process in this way, you develop muscle pathways that are not congruent with actual punches. Pulling needs to be deleted from your mindset and substituted for accuracy and control. Often the question arises, "What should a student focus on speed, power, or accuracy first?" The answer is accuracy, as even the slowest and weakest student can stand a chance of surviving an attack if their defence is on target.

In producing power through the body in the manner described above, you must have a switch of thoughts. There are arts, which teach many moves, compounded upon each other, and part of the reason for this is that if the first strike does not work, then you can move on quickly to the next and then the next, until the outcome is successful. There is nothing wrong with this, but it can lead to a negative thought process where your moves are deemed not successful. It is more positive to change your thought process to the fact that every strike works perfectly. That will never happen of course and we should always prepare for the next move, but at least it allows us to look at a power strike in a way that is congruent with what will happen when the strike is successful (visualisation!). Take the reverse punch: executing the punch exactly as described earlier, your timing is perfect and the angle, torque, backup mass and bracing angle all come together at the right moment. So what should happen from the attacker's point of view? It would be like them running straight into a moving battering ram. They will react by moving away from the pain. This is the way it should be thought about: if you use complete control in the delivery of your punch, maintaining all the points above, this will protect you and your joints. The attacker's body moves away from the strike, but you do not move your weapon away from the attacker, unless a different method of delivery is used. This means that once your power has been transferred to your attacker and they have reacted in the correct manner, your fist will be in a new position, away from your body and extended. This becomes your new point of origin where you can move from rather than re-chambering to a different position, unless of course you choose to re-chamber after the punch is completed.

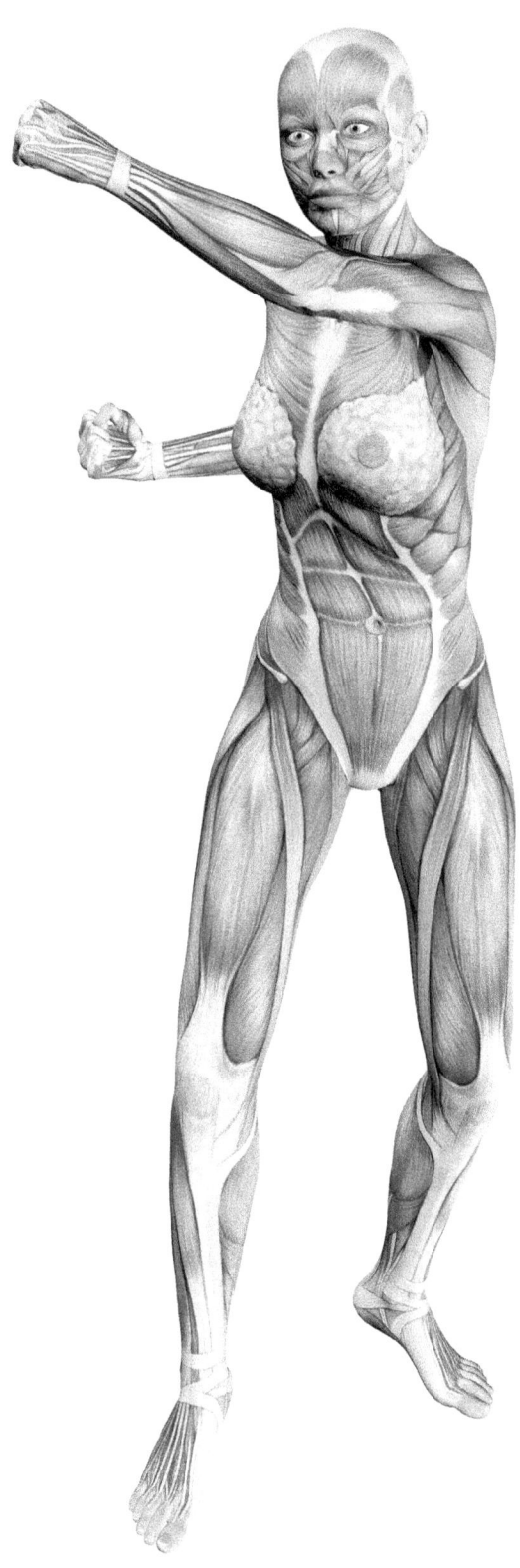

# 5 EFFECTIVE BLOCKS

Are blocks used within a martial application effective and efficient? There are four levels of effectiveness within a martial art that can be applied to moves: ineffective, effective, more effective, and most effective. It's not until we understand and analyse our moves with an open and impartial mind that we are able to come to grips with the moves in our own particular art and to be able to study those from different arts.

SECTION 5.1

# ANATOMICAL ALIGNMENT

Blocks are considered the mainstay of the majority of arts taught today. They are one of the first lessons taught to a new student. We're going to explore their effectiveness, how do they work, and what's happening as they are being performed. There are four basic blocks that are taught within the Martial Arts today, whatever the art or system a version of each of these blocks may be included in the training, they may be different in their delivery and end position, but in general they will be the same.

They are: upward (blocking something coming at you from a high zone), inward (blocking something coming to you from your left side and high), outward (something coming at you from you right side high), and downward (something coming at you from a low zone), whatever block is executed with the right can also be done with the left. Any block has to be effective or else the block is useless. If the arm that you put up to stop an incoming punch is not up to the task, the punch will continue on its way and strike its target. If that's your head, you are already on a slippery slope to getting hurt.

A block has several different segments to it, such as how it gets to the required position, the specific part of the arm being used to block, muscle structure, direction, and the internal skeletal structure. With any block, the angle that the arm takes to resist the force coming towards the head is also important, as the angle of the arm and forearm is part of the alignment of the block. In 4.4, I introduced the 180 degree point. This is the relationship of the arm to the forearm when it is locked out straight. Any bend at the elbow will result in a change in this relationship and will result in an angle being created.

There are two terms to help us understand angles regarding the position of the arm: acute and obtuse. Any angle between 0 and 90 degrees is acute and any angle between 90 and 180 degrees is obtuse, as shown below.

The angle relationship is one part; the next is the rotation and position of the fist and forearm. Any angle that the arm can position itself in can be affected by rotation of the fist and forearm. This is very important as the rotation of the two bones within the forearm can misalign a block that might be at its optimum angle for resisting force and so render it less effective. This means that the angle and rotation of the arm, fist and forearm have a direct relationship to each other to ensure the block used is at its most effective.

Let's look at the way the muscles work to keep structure in the arm when the hand is rotated around the wrist. The Pronator Quadrates are the main muscles involved in the twisting and torque action of the forearm, which is known as pronation. If you hold your hand out in front of you with your palm facing up and then go through the movement of pronation, you will move your hand through 180 degrees of rotation so that the hand is now palm down.

These two pictures show the rotation of the hand through 180 degrees.

Let's now ascertain which position of the arm is the most effective in resisting force when applied against an incoming punch.

There are three basic positions:

1, When the palm of the hand is facing you.

2, When the palm of the hand has been turn through 180 degrees and is now facing away from you.

3, When the hand is half way between the above two positions, or 90 degrees in the rotation.

To discover the strongest and most aligned position of the arm required to resist a punch, let's try another experiment. We are looking for resistance in a particular situation, which in this case is a punch coming toward your head at a high level. Before we can get to the testing of the hand and forearm position within a block, we must set the base structure of the body.

Assume a dimensionally accurate right neutral bow stance, using the right arm as the blocking arm and having the right foot forward. Position the left hand as a closed fist, bent high on your left side, fist under and behind the left peck muscle. With the right arm at your side, lift your arm up in front of you, bending the arm and forearm; to create a 130 degree angle, the right fist should be opposite your left shoulder, palm facing the ground, your arm will now be level on a horizontal plane. Ensuring that you maintain the same 130 degree angle between the forearm and your upper arm, rotate the right arm clockwise, so that your forearm is now vertical and your palm is facing you, your elbow should remain at the same height as your right shoulder. Now lift the arm higher and move it so that the arm is now on the 1.30-7.30 line, keeping the forearm vertical and lifting it higher you will automatically maintain the 135-degree angle between the forearm and the upper arm. Now rotate the fist through 90 degrees and drop the arm ensuring that the elbow does not fall below the shoulder joint. You have now created an anatomically aligned block with your right arm. The last part to set is the attack. Assume that the attack is a punch with your attacker's left fist. The punch is a wide swinging roundhouse punch aiming for your head. Due to this being a circular punch, the direction of the force at the point of impact will be from your right side at a 45-degree angle, so this is the direction that force will be applied to your block, shown in the next sequence of pictures. If we take a section of the arm from the shoulder and look at the angle from a different perspective, the angle that we have created is 135 degrees as in the picture below. There is a degree of play in this position, which can be between 145 and 135 degrees. Viewing this position from 1:30, you will see complete alignment from the right fist through the forearm, arm, right shoulder, left shoulder, right and left hip, down through the left leg to the rear foot and into the ground. The right leg also follows the same alignment. You are now in position for the experiment.

Experiment 6:

1. Move your arm into the position described above, following the instructions. With your palm facing you, and your fist closed, tense all the muscles that you can to support your right arm, and do not allow it to bend when force is applied. Have a second person take up a position at 1:30 on the clock facing your arm, placing their left hand in the bend of your right elbow and their

right hand against the back of your right fist. Applying force, they must gradually try to bend your fist in towards your head and you have to resist, as the last picture below demonstrates.

2. Repeat the movement of your arm again, ensuring that you maintain the above end position, turn your fist through 180 degrees so that the back of your hand is facing you, apply force.

3. Repeat the movement again, this time rotate the fist through 90 degrees, so that your thumb is facing you, apply force.

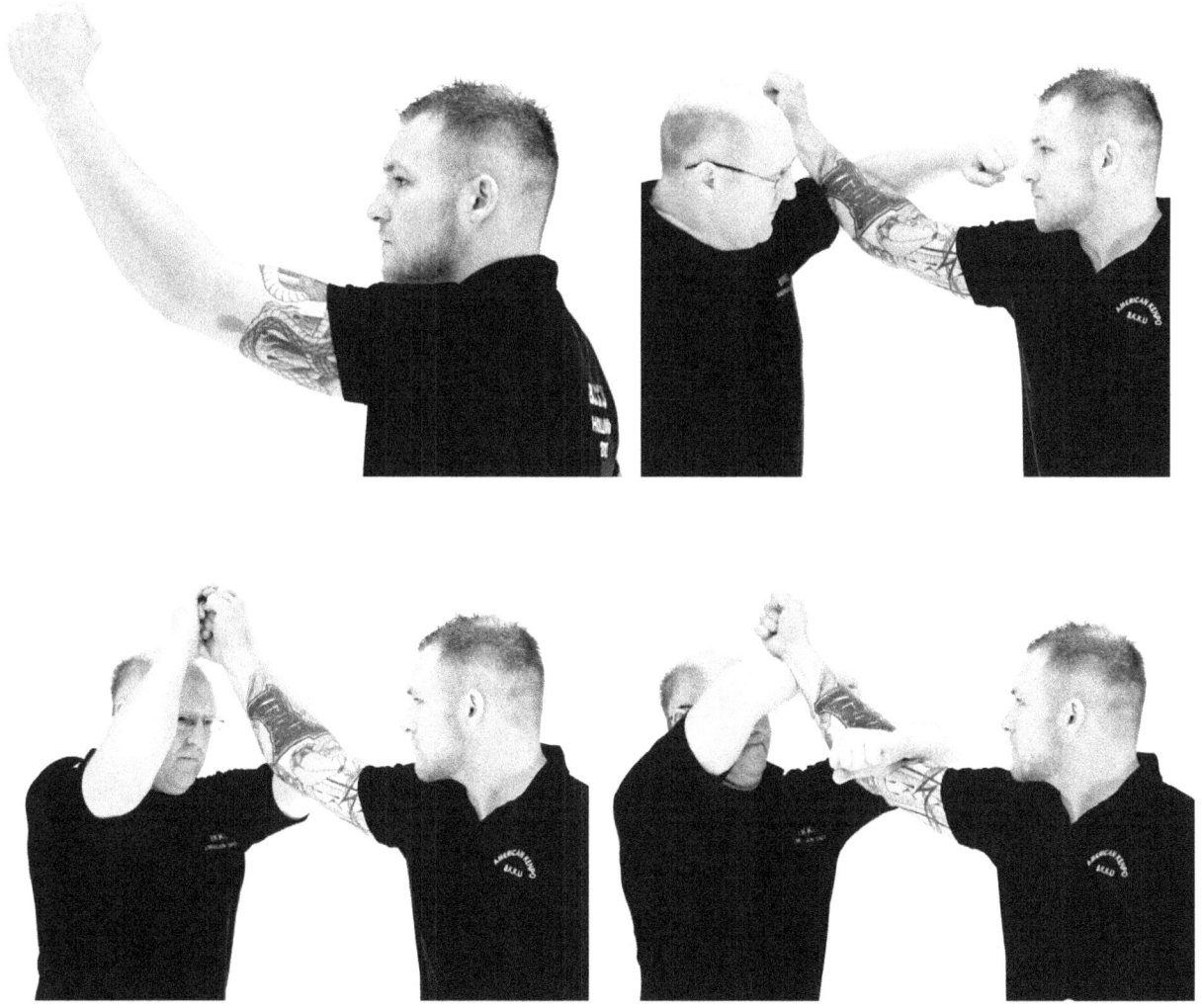

Repeat the above resistance test on each of the above 3 fist positions, ensuring constant force is being applied. Between each test, the person doing the block should reset the arm each time and rotate to the position required for the test. This creates a constant fresh starting position rather than just leaving the arm up and moving the fist. It is important to remember that it's not the person applying the force who needs to feel the strength of each position; it's the person doing the block. Repeat the test several times and then change partners. What you will feel and find is that you are capable of resisting force applied much easier when the fist has taken up position 3 above. The person applying the force will also notice a marked change in the amount of force needed to affect the bend in the arm. The most aligned and stable position for a blocking arm is with the fist aligned as in section 3 above. You will also find from engaging all the muscles that the arm and supporting muscles work better with the fist aligned in this manner. You have in this simple test found correct body alignment. This test and block alignment was introduced by (Chapél).

Just lifting the arm to the position to stop an incoming punch is not enough. The correct biomechanics need to be followed to create a solid structure, one that can stop a punch, delivered with a high degree of force. There are ways to move the arm to take up this position at the point of contact with the punch that are not biomechanically correct. Repeat the above experiment, this time just lift the arm into position, instead of going through all the above movements. Any blocking movement needs to be in time or just in front of your attacker's punch to work, it's the degree of efficiency and effectiveness, which is important.

When looked at from a third person's perspective, they should see all the mechanics of the body in a dimensionally accurate stance with an anatomically aligned block, as shown in the above picture.

Having your body aligned correctly behind your blocking arm is of utmost importance to ensure that the block used to stop an incoming punch is going to be at its most efficient and effective.

Blocks are one of the first weapons in your arsenal, but in so many cases they are ineffective when pressure tested against a punch, which is intended to hurt. Finding the balance between protecting a student from being hurt in the school and not giving them effective tools to protect themselves on the street is a decision, which only the instructor can decide upon.

SECTION 5.2

# UPWARD BLOCK

An upward block is often referred to as a roof block and can be taken to mean exactly that. You place the arm above your head in the same manner as a roof to stop an overhead attack. Yet often there is a mistaken understanding of what is actually required. The description is only a visual reference to help the student understand the block.

From a horse stance, position the arm above the head in the shape of a roof with the fist closed and over your centre line, as the following picture shows.

This position is sometimes supported by your other arm and is called an overhead cross block. Let's look at the psychology and the biomechanical issues behind this block. First we have the attack to consider, as in the block's description, we are blocking something coming at you from over the top of your head, hence the name and position of the block, the problem with this type of application is that unless something is falling out of the sky, it's not going to be effective! You are never going to be attacked in this way; the biomechanics of the attack will not work. One of the most popular attacks that this block is used against is an overhead club attack, so let's have a look at the biomechanics of this attack, as understanding this will prepare our minds for the adjustments necessary to achieve effectiveness with the upward block.

With a club in their right hand, the attacker has their left foot forward and steps through with their right foot. As they do, they swing the stick in a large arc over their head with the intention of bringing the club down on the top of your head. Notice the attack follows a large circular arc. Analysing the path of the attack along with the direction of delivery and the angle that the strike is traveling in, will result in a degree of force being applied behind the strike on a downward angle.

There is also an amount of forward force and inertia. Within the circle or path of action there are several segments that the strike/stick has to pass through to complete the whole path of action. Breaking the circle down into quadrants, it is possible to determine the path of travel throughout the whole movement. Say that the stick lies on the ground behind the attacker. He bends down, lifts the stick and immediately begins his attack. His arm is straight and so the fulcrum of the circle is the attacker's shoulder. With the tip of the stick leaving the floor, the first quarter of the path sees the point of the stick traveling forward and upward, reaching an apex above the head.

The second part of the circle sees the stick traveling forward and down. This means that the effect of this type of attack on the upward block will not be as effective as it could be, as the block is only designed to redirect force from above and not deflect any forward inertia as shown in the previous picture.

The segment of the circle intended to be the impact part is the second quarter of the circle, therefore we must address this block in a slightly different way, as the attack is not only from above, it also has some forward momentum. To enable this block to be effective against an overhead attack, the block has to address two angles of attack at once instead of blocking on a single dimension, i.e. downward only. It must become a two dimensional block, deflecting and resisting force and inertia from a downward direction as well as a forward direction; angling the block forward does this.

From the above description of a roof block, it is relatively easy to find the more effective position. Take the fist that is above your head, point it to 10.30, and rotate the forearm through a

45 degree turn, the forearm now faces 10:30. This will reduce the centre line coverage the block affords. To compensate for this, move the fist towards 10:30, this will bring your bicep close to your head. Notice the angle created with the arm and forearm is the same angle used for an inward block. This creates the necessary angle to deflect the overhead attack safely.

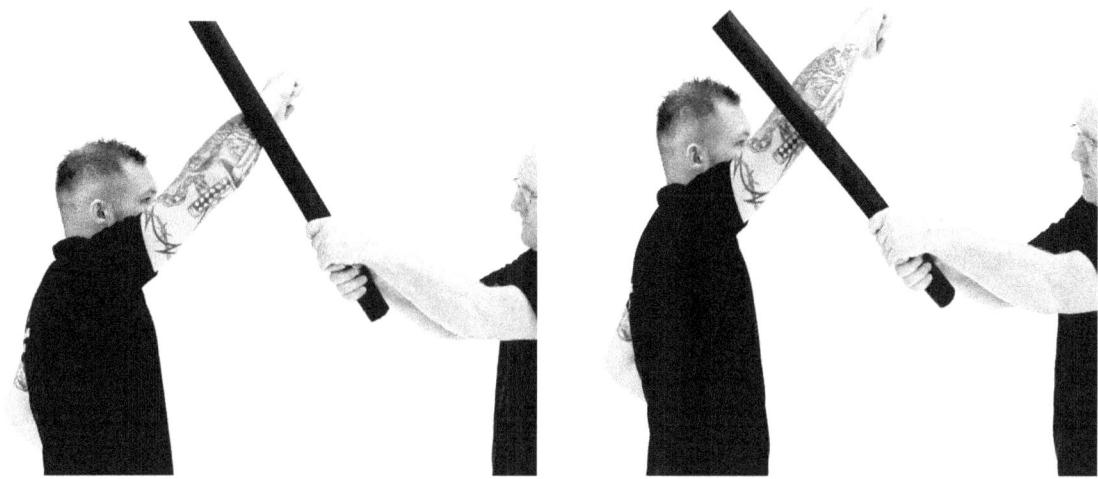

SECTION 5.3

# INWARD BLOCK

This block is one of the most effective blocks in this family group. It has farther to travel to get to its optimum position, but once there it will afford your high zone a great deal of protection and stability. It is easily misunderstood and is often executed in ways that make it as close to ineffective as you can get within a martial application. When performed correctly, the reason for the effectiveness of this block becomes apparent, the effectiveness lies in its anatomical alignment and path of travel.

Take up a dimensionally accurate right neutral bow stance. Ensure that your right arm creates the same angle as in 5.1 at 135 degrees. With the right arm at your side, begin to move the arm backwards in a large circular orbit, once the movement has been started create the alignment angle of 135 degrees. Your arm should fully rotate through all of your shoulder movement, as you begin to bring the arm down, you should be hammering with your fist towards 10.30 on the clock. Ensure that you stop the movement when your right elbow drops to the same height as your shoulder. Viewing this position from 10:30, you will see complete alignment from the right fist through the forearm, arm and right shoulder, which creates a 90-degree angle with your left shoulder, right and left hip, down through the left leg to the rear foot and into the ground. The right leg also follows the same alignment.

The most important movement with the execution of this block is the complete rotation of your shoulder joint. If you were to lift the arm into position you will not create the same anatomical alignment of all the supporting shoulder muscles that are gained from the biomechanical movement of the whole shoulder when the rotation is used. A key understanding with this move is, that the great majority of attacks are punches to the head, therefore it is really important to ensure that any block designed to protect the head meets two primary goals: -

1. The arm and its position are strong enough to withstand the amount of force being applied.

2. The arm is positioned high enough to ensure that any punch, at whatever height and angle of attack will be stopped.

These two primary goals are required to ensure that you are able to survive the initial attack, which then enables you to execute an effective counter. The blocking area of the arm should be the whole forearm, from your wrist to your elbow.

SECTION 5.4

# CONGRUENCY

The word congruence, from the Latin "congruere," means to come together, agree. As an abstract term, it means the similarity between objects and implies a relationship between angles. They are isometric (equal in measure); if they are the same shape and size they are congruent. In a martial application, you can interpret congruence in a way that is directly related to the alignment of the blocks above, or in terms of practicing your moves in a way in which they are more likely to be used in a live situation. The difficulty is having an understanding of live situations and teaching moves that are practical or congruent with the environment for which they are designed.
Many students are taught their moves from the horse stance. There is nothing wrong with using

this stance as a training horse stance, yet it is not a congruent stance in its application of the moves taught. You can stand in a horse stance all day long and perfect the moves required, but if you are ever in a situation which calls for you to block a punch, it's just about guaranteed that you will not be in a horse stance when the punch is being thrown, which makes the practicing of these moves from the horse stance incongruent. Congruency is an important consideration within practical applications in the martial arts.

We've studied the alignment principles of inward and outward blocks and gained an understanding of the angle applied to the arm and forearm. This is the primary angle that should be applied to most blocks. If you view this in a slightly different way, you will see the relationship to certain shapes. With the shoulder as a reference point, draw a line between the fist and the shoulder to create a triangle. This is one of those shapes that if maintained in the same position becomes a congruent shape. If you constantly change the shape and position of your blocks, the result is incongruent angles. When teaching a new student, one of the aims is to create muscle pathways so the beginner picks up the moves quickly and is able to apply these after short periods of training. But how can this happen if, when teaching, there is no constant reference point for the body to remember? That is exactly why I am putting forward this point now. Once you understand the above obtuse angle and the importance of congruency, your body will ingrain these moves much quicker rather than having different positions for a great variety of blocks.

The four blocks below maintain the same 145-degree angle and are therefore congruent with each other. Understanding congruency is the first part of this equation; the next is being able to obtain the congruent angle from any given position and that's the hard part. The first step to the creation of this angle is to learn the execution slowly, finding the angle and then maintaining it throughout your movement. The four blocks are not the only ones to which this angle is applicable. It can be used in most of the major blocks, plus a few others that are not so obvious until they are pointed out. This makes the angle described above truly congruent.

The pictures below show all 4 major blocks. The Inward, Outward Extended, Downward and Upward.

SECTION 5.5

# **BLOCK OR STRIKE**

The application of blocks, the biomechanics behind their delivery, and the alignments obtained when the moves are executed, do create a very strong appendage. It also completely depends upon the intended use of your arm whether it is a block or a strike. When used as a block, the arm is capable of stopping a large amount of force coming behind the punch. Reversing that thought process, the block also becomes a very effective strike.

Thinking outside the box, these moves can also be used as weapons to cause breaks, as they are very hard to collapse. If you can manipulate an attacker's arm into a position where force can be applied through your aligned position, the breaking of or serious hyperextension of the limb is a relatively easy outcome, especially if the limb has been extended and downward force is applied. The difference between a block and a strike is found within your intent and how quick the initial move is executed. If you are caught off guard then a block or shield may be your first line of defence. If you are prepared then the block can easily be seen as an offensive block. Thus becoming an offensive defence, rather than simply a defence.

All the above blocks that have been covered can be applied in either a defensive or an offensive manner, depending upon your circumstances at the time of execution. Ensuring that the weapons or blocks are aligned correctly will result in a more effective and efficient means of execution, quite often when taken in the context of a martial application, speed is seen as the primary goal, at the cost of effectiveness and efficiency. However it is of no use employing a weapon or block with speed and then as a result of this, not being able to stop the incoming attack.

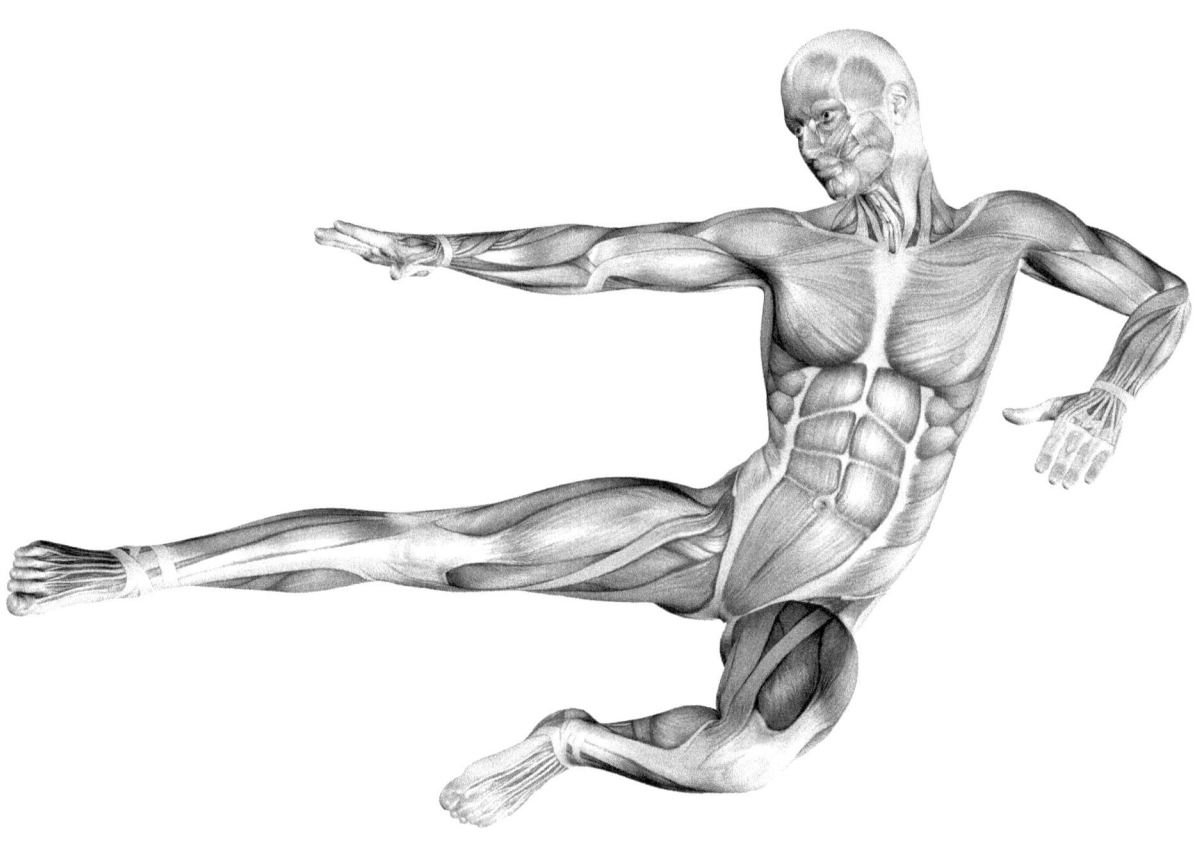

# 6 CORRECT ANATOMICAL KICK ALIGNMENT

The martial arts are known for their kicks, especially high kicking techniques. Yet how many times have you heard, "High kicking is great but can you step back and kick someone in a crowded bar?" In some environments, high kicking is simply not practical. Just walking down the street you'll often find the pavement or ground is uneven and it's hard to maintain balance when lifting a leg into the air, especially when trying to execute high kicks. The stage for high kicking is usually reserved for tournaments.

SECTION 6.1

# PRACTICAL AND SAFE

If you are in a confined space, trying to kick an attacker in the head will not be the most effective technique. It may be counter-productive and unsafe for you to attempt such a skilled maneuver, meaning it may not be physically safe to continually perform high kicks over long periods of time. When children are developing and learning how to coordinate their bodies, teaching them high kicks can easily damage muscle, ligaments and joints. As you get older, the ability for joints to lubricate themselves diminishes, while muscle shortens and becomes less resistant to high, fast movement, often causing strains and pulls.

Let's look at the types of movement associated with kicking and their applications, along with some normal biomechanical movement. The most obvious place to start is kicking a ball. This again is one of those activities, which so many do without thought as to which actions the body has to go through to perform a standard ball kick. The first point to consider is, is kicking a ball an aligned movement? When football players in Europe kick a ball, the leg swing created for the kick has an arching action that takes the leg from one side across in front of the pelvic bone. The leg does not follow the natural alignment of a walking motion. Even if the leg is swung in an anatomically aligned arch, the foot position is changed on impact. If it is not changed, you get a toe punt, which does not give the ball control required. In American football, the leg action is completely different. The leg swing occurs while in the natural alignment of the walking arch, then follows through the kicking point, this action pulls the other leg off the ground due to the amount of inertia created by the kicking leg. It is aligned with the pelvic bone and does not swing across the body. In most cases, the kicking leg is straightened at the point of impact and the knee does not travel much higher than waist level.

Going back to that sprinter mentioned earlier in the book, the one using asymmetrical movement: he is in a way performing a kicking action every time the leg is powered forward. The knee is the first part of the driving force, followed by the extension of the lower leg, all in alignment with the hips. There are many different ways to kick in the martial arts. Choosing a safe and practical way is not as easy as it sounds unless you stick to a very simple rule: kick in a way that is aligned to your biomechanical structure.

SECTION 6.2

# ALIGNMENT

The difficulty with alignment and kicks is that keeping alignment reduces the amount of kicks down from an untold number to just four. That doesn't mean these four kicks can't be used in a variety of ways, but for some, this is too great a reduction from what they are already doing. Any kick should follow the movement and relationship between the leg and the pelvic bone. The key here is the hip joint; this is a ball and socket joint, and as such it has a great range of movement. Unlike the shoulder joint, the hip spends the majority of its time moving in a particular sequence and is a good example of NMP. If we play sports requiring us to move and use the legs in a manner that is different from our everyday activity, then movement training is required. This is not necessarily aligned movement. When we walk from the car to the house, or from the car to the shopping centre, it's usually in a straight line. We don't walk sideways or backwards. This means that over a lifespan, the ball and socket joint of the hip gets programmed into this movement. All muscles, tendons, and nerves are used to support this action.

Therefore the most natural of all kicks is going to be the front kick. This kick is not the same as the one used to kick a ball. This kick uses the relationship between the thigh and the lower leg to create the action of a kick found in martial arts. Assuming the training horse stance described in 1.2, lift your knee in front of you no higher than your hip and make sure the lower leg maintains its vertical alignment and the foot stays engaged. Do not let the foot drop so that the toes point towards the ground, as shown in the picture a, keep the foot engaged as in picture B.

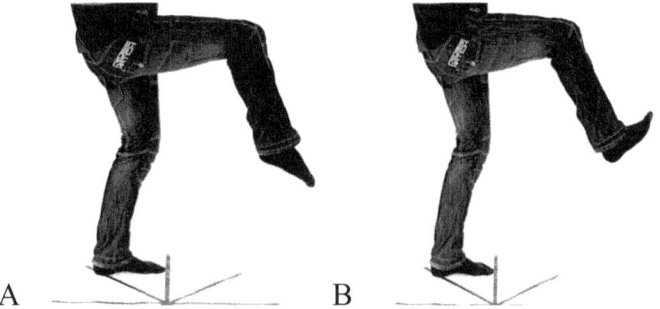

Providing that the thigh is horizontal to the ground, you can now execute the movement of the kick. Understanding alignment and biomechanics allows you to see how this kick is aligned, not only from the movement created by the knee and lower leg, but also by the natural NMP movement of the thigh. The whole walking procedure is aligned, so this makes the front kick the most aligned kick. Now for two other martial arts kicks: the round kick and the sidekick. Both kicks require movement that is outside of the walking gait. The round kick requires you to rotate the leg from the hip joint and throw the kick in towards your centre line, much like a roundhouse punch. Unless you have spent a reasonable amount of time stretching the muscles and ligaments of the lower platform, the rotating action of the leg will force the upper body to lean away from the kick, which affects the power being delivered, and the posture and balance of the body. The other problem that is created by this action is the effect on the lower leg joints. Both the supporting knee and ankle are being put under a lot of stress. There are many ways in which the lower leg is used to support and generate this type of kick, such as turning the supporting leg and foot all the way round, resulting in the foot pointing in completely the opposite direction to which the kick is being thrown.

The pictures below demonstrate the twisted mechanics of this type of roundhouse kick. The hip joint in this action becomes the pivotal point, with all the body mass going in one direction and the kicking leg going in the other direction.

The forces are completely out of line with the direction of the kick with the majority of the mass not supporting the kick, the alignment is also abnormal. The second method of executing this kick has its own biomechanical problems. This time the supporting foot does not change its position in such a drastic manner. It is either kept facing the direction of the kick or moved and placed so that the foot faces the 10:30. This in itself is not the wrong angle; what makes this contrary to our body movement is the way the kick is executed, with the upper body rotated around the hip joint in the opposite direction to where the foot is facing while throwing the kick in the opposite direction to which the upper body rotates. This kick can be executed with a certain amount of power, as your upper body causes torque to help you launch the kick. You pull in one direction and kick in another. The problem here is that the movement is not aligned with the natural movement of the spinal column, hip and knee joint. They are all being subjected to rotational twisting forces, especially the knee. Not only is the knee having to support the weight of the body, it is also receiving all the rotational force being delivered by the upper body. It is not designed for this and over time damage will occur. There is no alignment or biomechanical movement.

Teaching movement in this manner while executing these two kicks is not efficient and certainly not within NMP parameters. Learning to kick in this way can be termed, 'learned bad behaviour'. The sidekick is also no better; the difference with this kick is that the hip joints are being forced apart as the sidekick is thrown. Both the roundhouse and the sidekick are mechanically unsound. We must perform these in a biomechanically aligned manner to get the best efficiency from the two kicks. To help understand the alignment principles of the roundhouse kick, it must be altered slightly to gain better effectiveness. Kicking someone in the head is not effective in an aligned manner without complete freedom of the hip joint.

From a dimensionally accurate left neutral bow stance as outlined in 1.4, lift the forward left foot from its position facing 1:30 and replace the foot facing 10:30. Now transfer your mass over the foot. At all times during the execution of this kick, ensure that the planted left foot remains stable and fixed in position. When this is achieved, lift the rear foot. While your leg is within the swing movement, keep the lower leg and the thigh at a 90-degree angle, while the knee continues through the swing and reaches 1:30 on your clock. It is at this point or slightly before, that the lower leg flexes and the foot begins its path to contact. The kick should not travel through the target (it is akin to the back fist), as contact is made, the foot recoils to its reference position just before the execution of the kick and the knee remains in its position in space. When the kick is completed and the foot returns to its starting point, the forward foot is planted down.

Throughout the execution of this kick, the right hip is being brought through its natural arch, but should not go beyond the 1:30 reference point. This will mean that when the foot is planted to the ground at the 1:30 point, the knee and hip will already be at this angle. You should be able to plant the foot immediately, without any adjustment, taking up a dimensionally aligned right neutral bow stance.

The following pictures show the accurate footwork, of the roundhouse kick.

Side-Blade Kick

The alignment associated with this kick is no different from the round kick, the only difference is the execution of the kick from the knee reference point. From this point the lower leg extends and the foot kicks out towards 1:30 using the side or the heel to contact the target. It then plants towards 1:30 and you end up in the same stance as above.

A great deal of kicks performed in the martial arts arena are potentially contrary to our natural biomechanical movement. We must be aware of the stresses and strains put on the human body when executing certain kicks. There is a definite difference between what are effective aligned kicks against misaligned ineffective kicks. When we practice on the heavy bag, it soon becomes apparent how some kicks are completely ineffective. While executing aligned kicks we need to use solid principles of biomechanics to help make them work.

SECTION 6.3

# SPEED OR POWER KICKS

Kicks come in two basic variations: those using speed as part of their effectiveness and those requiring backup mass or thrust to cause a certain effect. The round kick is a hybrid using both speed and power, applied in a circular motion.

Power has a very different effect than speed, when contact is made, the leg does not recoil because the intention is, that the target moves away from the kick. The leg is kept tight by the tensing of the major muscles of the leg on impact. Though the result looks very powerful, as long as the target moves away from the impacting kick, then there is no problem. If the leg has a stable mass, the leg can be put under a great deal of pressure that is absorbed through the joints. This type of kick can be effective though it is not aligned or efficient.

Let's compare the intended outcome of a speed kick as opposed to a power kick and the biomechanical differences between them. The obvious difference is the speed at which they are delivered. The speed of a snapping kick can be applied effectively in three kicks: the front, side, and the round with all relying on the lower leg moving at speed to the target and then returning to its point of origin, much like the snapping back fist described earlier. Only two of these three kicks can be used for power and speed.

With the front snapping kick, the knee is raised, ensuring that the upper leg is horizontal to the ground. The most important part of the biomechanics of this move is to ensure the hip on the side that you are kicking with is held back as the kick is thrown. As the kick is using speed to create its effectiveness, it should be executed with efficiency by ensuring the pelvic bone maintains its alignment with your upper torso and shoulders. To be able to do this, the kick has to be executed from a stable balanced posture with 100% of your weight on your supporting leg. If you allow the hip to travel beyond the point described above, your posture will be affected and you run the risk of losing balance and the kicking leg pulling the body forward.

The two pictures below show the hip being held back, the leg does not fully extend.

Speed is the required movement; therefore the target chosen should be compatible with your action. The main aim of this type of technique is to keep your attacker within range. Fast snapping techniques are used to ensure that the attacker remains within your field of combat, rather than moving them away. If you have chosen to use this type of technique, it is very important that you have another move ready.

The power kick, or thrusting kick, uses the principles of power generation such as backup mass, rotational torque, and gravitational marriage. Correct alignment is needed for effective technique. Backup mass is not so easy when you are trying to create this from a kick, so movement is of paramount importance. Power and inertia are not obtainable unless you are moving forward at the same time you throw the kick. The biggest change in the action of the kick is that a thrust cannot be achieved from the same mechanics as a snapping kick because there is no alignment or momentum. To execute a thrusting kick, the knee has to be lifted higher than the target. As you straighten the leg, the pelvic bone tilts to support the thrust. The key is to make sure that the thrusting of the hips, straightening of the leg, and the momentum required all come together at the point of impact. When this is achieved, the result on your attacker is usually very effective, causing them to move violently away from the encounter.

The above pictures above show a thrusting action and the momentum that is created with this type of kick.

With the snapping kick, the body weight is centered over the hips and the supporting leg. When the thrusting kick is executed, the body is moving and the leg is in front of the hips. The only option if this kick is thrown correctly is to step forward and regain your balance. The inertia and momentum follows through the kicking movement. Timing is very important because if your timing is out when impact is expected, you will have no choice other than to step forward.

Having explained the snap and the thrust, it's now possible to see that the round kick follows different principles. When the kick hits its target and stays there, no follow through with back up mass is produced, it can be executed with a snap, but quite often it is used to produce power, yet lacks the principles needed to achieve an effective technique.

SECTION 6.4

# KNEES AND THE KICKING PROCESS

When using the front kick, we have all the alignment that we need to create a biomechanically aligned kick. For safety I have chosen not to explain a high kick when the target is the head. It is not effective to use a thrust kick high, as the knee has to be lifted higher than the target. This kick can be executed but does require a degree of training and skill to pull it off because the thrust and angle are very difficult to achieve.

Using a snapping action to perform a high kick is more efficient than the thrust. When the knee is lifted to a horizontal position and executed, the target will be in line with the knee. The knee acts as an aiming position; wherever the knee is pointed and a snapping kick is executed, the foot will go to that point. This is not the same with the thrusting kick, due to the knee having to be higher and then dropping as the kick is executed. With a snapping kick, the knee joint works within its natural movement. Every time we take a step, we perform the same action, almost as if every step is a mini kick. A safety consideration to note: the knee joint works like a hinge; it will not allow further movement once the leg is locked out. If we consider this fact and then analyse the force applied to the knee, if the follow through round kick is used, the conclusion is that the knee joint is put under tremendous pressure when impact occurs. Continued repetition on a heavy bag results in the knee being damaged because the joint is not made to work in this manner. There is no body alignment with this action and certainly no NMP, so great care should be taken when teaching this kick.

Thrusting or snapping the lower leg out when performing the sidekick is very akin to a thrust punch. The leg is extended to its limit and the knee is continually straightened. Great care needs to be taken to ensure that lock out does not happen; if it does then damage will happen over time. Whenever this move is used, you should always slightly bend the knee. If you expend all the power in the lock out, your leg only has one way to move, backwards in the bending action. Any strike should ensure that it has penetration left within the muscles of the limb being used, the knees are no different.

SECTION 6.5

# FOOT ALIGNMENT IN PROPRIORCEPTION

The foot is the one part of our body that continuously takes impact. Every time you take a step, the foot experiences the force of the impact and then supports all the weight of the body as you transition through your walking gait. The heel takes the brunt of any force. The ball of the foot allows the transference of the weight and the final flexing of the toes to propel the body into its next step.

If we look at which part of the foot is the natural part to take impact in a kick, the conclusion is the heel. So why is it that thrusting heel kicks are not more common within the martial arts? They are used with such kicks as spinning heel kicks and axe kicks but not when kicking forward.

The reason is that if you were to use the heel, you would have to lock out the leg to obtain the right angle for the heel to make contact with the target, and the higher the kick, the harder it is to bring the heel into play. If there was a target on the ground and you wanted to use the heel in a stomping action, you'll find the alignment much easier.

Rising up onto the balls of the feet is a relatively easy move, though it cannot be sustained for long. This alignment is exactly the same alignment used when executing the front kick, every bone and muscle in the leg are aligned, from the hip through the knee and finally to the ball of the foot. There are large forces applied through the foot, such as at the midpoint of our step. The compression at this point can be anything up to thirteen times the body's weight, executing a kick with correct alignment should be one of the most effective weapons we have. The natural alignment and posture that the foot creates while standing is another NMP link. We spend so much time standing on our feet, that it's not hard to see why it gets programmed in so quickly. This NMP position makes kicking with the ball of the foot second nature.

The sidekick is executed in a similar fashion to the hand sword, using the side of the foot as the weapon. Although at first this does seem like a natural progression (going from the side of the hand to the side of the foot), this weapon does not have a great deal of alignment to back it up, making this weapon vulnerable to over-extension. The foot has approximately 20% movement in the dorsiflexion range. If a sidekick is executed in a manner involving power generation (which means the involvement and use of inertia with backup mass) and good strong contact is made with a hard target, then you might find the alignment is off. If this is the case, a great deal of force will continue in the direction applied, causing a twist or strain of the ankle, just like when you plant your foot on an unstable surface and the ankle gives way.

The above four pictures show the execution of a side blade kick.

Using a sidekick in a snapping action is not as bad, as force is not the primary goal of the technique, yet if the foot is not aligned, damage can occur. In martial arts the top of the foot is used as a weapon, usually in relation to a round kick, pointing the toes and using the top part as the impact point. Providing that the impact of the kick is taken high up the foot close to the ankle, impact shouldn't be a problem. If the impact is closer to the toes, over-flexation can occur, pulling the muscles and tendons on the top of the foot. The alignment is close to that used in the front kick. The soles of the feet are major sensors in the Samatosensory system (SS). They constantly receive information about the surface you are moving on, the amount of weight distribution required to make a single step, helping to adjust your body's posture to maintain equilibrium. Consider when you last walked on ice or a slippery wet surface, notice how the muscles in the legs and feet automatically adjust the confidence in your step? You perceive that the ground is unstable and your body adjusts the length of your gait. All of this is possible due to the SS and as such, the feet have a major part to play in the execution of kicks. It's not just the foot being used as the weapon; it's the foot being used as support that is pivotal in the effectiveness of the kick. If the supporting foot senses instability of any kind in the planting, propulsion, or support of the body during the action of kicking, it will, without cognitive thought, adjust your body. This may result in the kick being ineffective. Understanding that the foot senses instability can help a martial artist when preparing to deliver a kick.

Let's have a look at the foot movement in detail when executing a step through round kick. I choose this kick due to the direction in which the force is delivered, but the same principles covered here are just as valid with any other kick. The right neutral bow fighting stance is the starting position. Both feet should face 10:30. The left leg is brought into the kick by swinging the leg through an arch to the point where the lower leg performs the kick. While standing in this stance, have your rear leg muscles engage themselves ready to propel the body. A slight bend in the supporting leg occurs, which transfers a small amount of weight to the rear leg. This allows you to lift and maneuver your forward foot. Lift the foot clear off the ground and replace it facing 1:30.

The following pictures show the lifting and specific placing of the supporting leg.

To ensure the SS receives the correct information, place the foot on the ground with authority. This makes the SS tell the body that stability is needed. Another NMP point is that the foot should move forward toward the direction of travel. As the movement forward starts, the body weight transfers forward and into the supporting leg. Momentum begins and inertia follows. When this happens together, both the thought process and the senses of the body are correct, telling the body that forward motion is required and stability is necessary to perform a kick. Care needs to be taken to ensure the foot travels forward. If you move it either backward or sideways, a different NMP signal is sent to the brain. The kick will still be stable, but you will not be moving in your most efficient manner. When the foot has been re-engaged with the floor, the left kicking foot leaves the ground and is propelled around the hip in a swinging motion. Once the right and left hips reach their natural anatomically aligned position, the kick can be thrown. Stability should be found at this point, which will enable you to plant the forward foot with authority. The kick is delivered toward 1:30 the same direction that the supporting foot faces. The body will also be in a state of inertia, still moving forward, towards 1.30.

If stability is required after the kick is executed, then a stabilising mechanism is needed. This is the rear right foot performing a PAM, which will send those SS messages to the brain that the body has stabilised. All of this is inbuilt through the senses in the feet and the connection between the feet and NMP. If contact of the foot is made with your target, it will register immediately and your body will not require the previous stability.

# The Secret Science of Modern Martial Arts

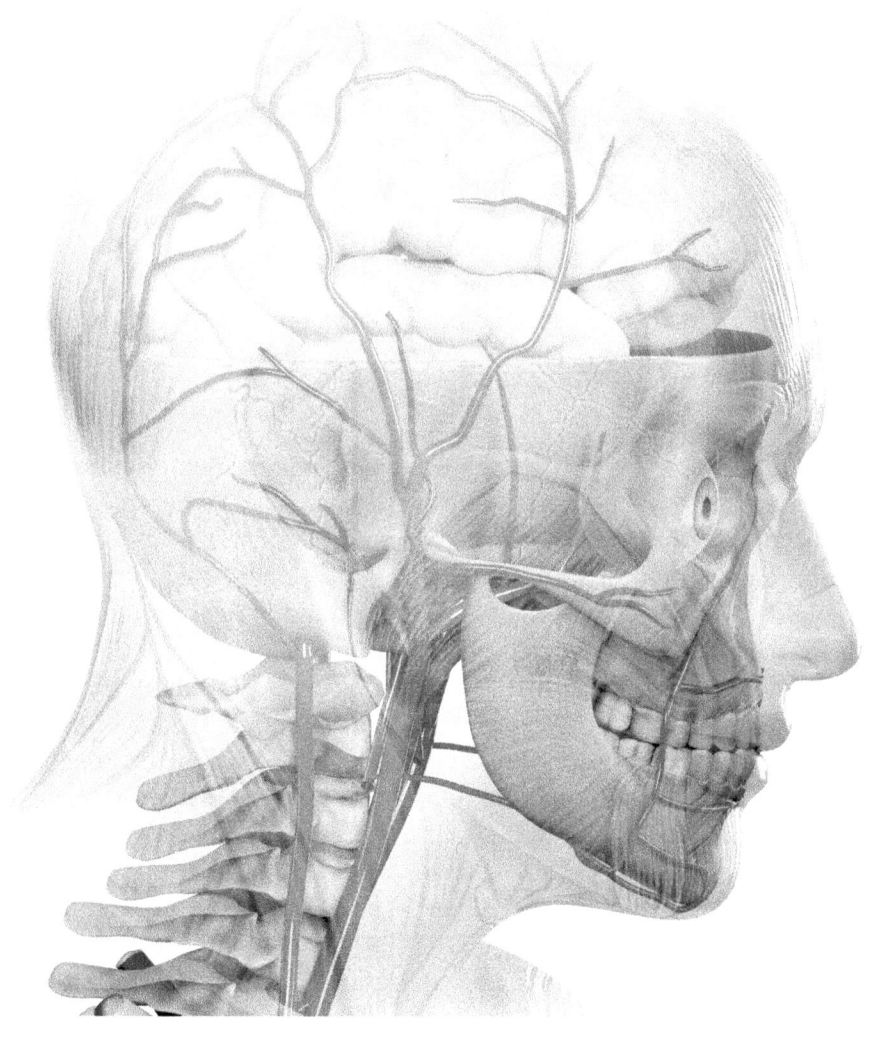

# 7 NEUROMUSCULAR PROGRAMMING

The approach to this subject is based upon the concept that the human body has evolved over thousands of years. During this time of development the brain and the body have come together to create a functioning system that is not only innate, but also completely synchronised to provide humans with effective and efficient means of movement.

SECTION 7.1

# THOUGHT PROCESS

In Chapter 2, section 2.1, I mentioned the Proprioceptive system. Let's explore this subject in more detail. Propriorception is the link between the body and the brain and creates awareness of posture, movement, and changes in balance. This system controls movement and allows the body to orient itself in space and time. Understanding this subject will make your martial art more effective.

Neuromuscular Programming (NMP) begins at birth and gradually over the years will build a direct link between the mind and the postures the body takes when moving through everyday life. Almost as soon as we begin to move as babies, NMP starts. Observe a baby grasping a finger or beginning to crawl: it spreads its hands to support its weight and crawls across the floor. As a young child, it may trip and fall toward the ground and automatically the hands spread in preparation for the impact that the body is expecting to encounter. An adult comes upon a large weight to push, so they open their hands and begin to push. Without any cognitive thought as to which body postures to assume, we learn them without being told. Nobody tells the young baby it needs to spread its hands to support its weight. Over the years, the posture of spreading your hands becomes so ingrained within your autonomic nervous system that cognitive thought does not happen. The programming between your mind and your body has already been created.

At this point it is almost impossible to tell what comes first. Your mind tells your body what to do and once your body follows the direction it has been given, the body reconfirms to the mind what posture has been created, they are inextricably linked together. Postures are created and in doing so you align your body behind the action. Your skeletal frame takes up a certain posture, which is supported by all the muscles, tendons, nerves, and fibres of your body needed to carry out the intended action, this is NMP. We walk and run without any consideration to the amount of information the mind and body must process to enable these functions. It is an impossibility to think about each movement needed to walk, let alone run. The same link between body and mind is found in just about every action that we do. When walking, the heel is placed on the ground and transfers weight, then the opposite leg swings and walks. NMP happens when the weight transfers from one foot to another. If you stand with both feet together and decide to walk, you transfer weight and engage the muscles of the supporting leg to push off. This transference and action is the body's way of recognising what action it has been called upon to perform. It has been programmed from the very first days when you started to stumble and walk. When you lift the knee to climb stairs, the same NMP kicks in. Our hands and the postures we assume with them play a large role in NMP. They are often used as a communication tool, i.e. shaking hands, waving goodbye, shaking your fist in anger, holding them up in front of you palms spread, they all have meaning and are automatically read by other people. These same postures have a direct effect when used in a martial application and understanding their relevance is of utmost importance. Let's look at hand postures in a little more detail to understand the basics of NMP.

Remember, it's the link between the posture and the action your mind has told your body to assume that we're looking at. Now imagine grasping a round door handle. This posture is very close to the one taken by the infant when it first grasps its parent's finger. Your mind knows that the handle has to rotate to open the door; it therefore forms a posture with your hand as you take hold of the handle and twist. The programmed position of your fingers and thumb around the handle, along with the hand position, the pressure touch sensors of the fingers and hand, back up the action of rotating the handle. The fingers spread and your metacarpals part, knowing you have to rotate. It also means your hand will take up an angle which will facilitate turning the handle. The action of rotation will stem from the torque of the horizontal axis; the muscles in your forearm and some support from your bicep create the kinetic motion.

Grasping a tall glass of water requires the same posture with the hand as above, but your intention is different. Instead of a rotating action, your mind is telling your arm that its primary intention is to lift. These two actions are very different and are transferred into many martial art techniques, usually when grabbing an attacker's limb.

Now let's look at the action of hooking or pulling, where the four fingers are together bracing each other. We use this posture when lifting a heavy table. The noticeable thing with this posture is the lack of use of the thumb. It does not form part of your hand structure in this action. If you wanted to support your body by way of a bar above your head, you would also use this same hand posture. The thumb works at its best when it is working in opposition to the index finger, allowing for very intricate manipulations to be performed. Try threading a needle with your small finger and your thumb and you will find that you don't have the fine motor control necessary to do it efficiently.

Here we have two distinct differences, one where the hand grasps something that allows for manipulation, while the other is for hooking and pulling. The thumb is the key, as seen in the picture below. With the grasping posture, the mind knows that the primary intention of the hand is to take hold of something and manipulate it. With the hooking posture, the mind is expecting a large degree of resistance force to be transmitted through the hand, resulting in two very different postures. This shows a direct link between the mind and the body. The postures we create have an influence on the effective action we want to perform. These postures, as well as the link to the brain, are programmed into us as we grow, creating NMP. These two very different postures and their adaptation were first introduced by Chapél (2001).

How does the understanding of these two postures and NMP help us within the martial arts? Let's look at applying these two hand postures within a technique; this will give you an opportunity to test how they feel when applied. As the hand postures are different, we must maintain a constant level of testing.

Experiment 7:

1. In a headlock, the attacker has put their right arm around your head. Just as they are about to apply pressure, you manage with your right hand to grab his right wrist. The grasp posture is very specific as described above and shown in the picture above. This can easily be set up in a safe environment without having to go through the motions of an attack. You stand still, allowing your partner to position their right arm.

2. Once in position and without applying force, grab his wrist with your right hand. Once you are both in your respective positions, the attacker will apply force gradually. As he does, you pull his right arm down and away from your neck. The key here is for you to feel the difference in applied force within your functional anatomy. Your partner needs to pay attention to the amount of effort required to ensure they maintain their position while you are trying to pull the arm down.

3. Reset the above position. It is important that you disengage from your partner and reapply the same position from the same reference point. Instead of grasping your partner's wrist, hook it as shown below.

Make sure that the thumb does not form part of the hook. The anatomical position of the major thumb muscle is not engaged, as it is when the grasp posture is used. Repeat the pull down test and above you will find that you are able to apply more pulling force with the hand when it is positioned in the hook posture. Part of the reason for this is the actual structure that the hand creates and the alignment of your muscles, bones and ligaments which all come into play to ensure that the desired action can be undertaken with efficiency. The flexor muscles of the fingers cross over several other joints in the hand. They are called Synergists and play an important role in preventing the wrist from moving. They allow for maximum power to be applied by the hand. Another reason for the difference in applied force is the link between mind and body, NMP. Each posture tells your mind and body something different. Both you and your partner can feel this. In the case of the experiment, if your intention within the first move is to survive the initial assault, you will need to use the most effective and efficient technique. As you have felt within the experiment, the hooking posture is more effective because it is in direct correlation to your NMP.

This is how important the understanding of body postures and NMP is. That very small change in your hand posture can make all the difference. Once you have survived the choke or strangle, you may want to manipulate you attacker's arm, so you must change hand postures to the grasp. If you don't, you will not be able to maintain control of the limb, as the hooking posture will not work when control is required.

SECTION 7.2

# STRIKING

When you form a posture that is intended as a weapon, NMP also comes into play. It does not matter which part of your body you use, the same thought process takes place. As you are preparing to fight, the body releases hormones designed to assist and support the intended action. When striking and getting into fight situations, the postures created to use as weapons have the added benefit of adrenaline and endorphins to help support the action.

The very action of forming a fist for example can start the process. If the body is not preparing for fight or flight, there is no real need for these two hormones to be released. Yet when you get into the mindset of fighting and form a fist aggressively, the posture you create activates your NMP and at the same time, due to the fact that the fist is an intended weapon, adrenaline and endorphins are released.

The posture, mind and hormones form a very natural proprietary state all due to the fist posture. Your fist is telling you that impact is imminent and as such the body requires endorphins to help the body cope with potential pain and the adrenaline to help all the other systems with the fight. I am not looking into the hormone effects in any depth here, just the links between NMP and the effects on our body. One of the things that martial arts are known for is kicking techniques; none more so than the front kick using the ball of the foot or the heel as the contact part. A kick is no more than an exaggerated step that employs the foot as a weapon. If you lift the leg and thrust it out to kick a door, you will automatically use the ball or the heel of the foot as the contact part. This is mainly because you walk using a heel-to-toe sequence. Every time the foot has an impact on the ground, it is supported by the theory of NMP, taking the impact of the placement and transferring this force through the body. This is programmed in from the very first time that we learn to walk. The programming is already built in to enable the foot to kick something; we simply have to change the method of execution slightly to make it effective.

Another link between the foot impacting the ground and NMP is stability, which is found within this part of the action. The body knows the heel being placed on the ground is the stabilising part of the gait, especially when the body is in normal walking mode. While the body is walking, it is in a state of falling, and when the heel contacts the ground, stability is restored.

SECTION 7.3

# CONTROL SYSTEMS

All the body's control systems are initiated through the central nervous system, an area of particular interest to NMP. Within this system is the Proprioceptive system, often referred to as the body's sixth sense. This system has several elements to it, with three directly related to human movement. These are the Samatosensory system (SS), vestibular system (VtS), and the visual system (VS). All play a part in human movement.

All movement we make has to have a starting place. It is the job of the three systems above to monitor and input sensory information regarding the body and its position and the space around us, including the surfaces we walk on. As we move and change our position, our environment also changes while at the same time our sensory systems are constantly monitoring everything from moment to moment. The majority of the changes made by these systems are without us being aware of them; they are completely automatic. It is these systems that are responsible for our protective responses, such as the startle reflex. Startle reflexes are responses from these systems. If we hear a gunshot go off close by, or a car backfiring, we are startled. When something comes close to your eyes, you blink or reflex your head away from the danger. If you step on something that causes pain or touch something hot, you pull the limb away. These startle reflexes are produced by the different monitoring sensory systems. We are aware of the five senses, yet these are incomplete without the Proprioceptive sense system.

Samatosensory System

The Samatosensory system provides our bodies with sensation feedback. It is responsible for telling us where each part of our body is in space and time and allows us to place our hands or legs into positions we cannot see directly. The system gathers its information from receptors found in our skin, muscles, tendons and joints. It allows us to distribute weight through our feet, judge and adjust the amount of pressure needed when gripping something, and judge the amount of weight or pressure needed to hold a limb in position when pressure is exerted. This system works automatically with no cognitive thought process, but can be used by experienced martial artists to disrupt the signals and trick the body into thinking that something is wrong or needs adjusting. Samatosensory is the key system that creates the NMP link. If we overlay the SS within certain postures, we discover that if the posture is expecting a certain reaction, the SS will confirm this.

When we were performing the pull and grasp experiment above, there was a difference in the amount of force which could be applied, which was due in part to this system sending back information that the body was indeed in the correct posture to apply a greater amount of force. One of the direct ways in which this system can be made active and used to our advantage is with the application of force to our attacker's body.

Experiment 8:

1. Have your partner stand naturally. Stand behind them, place your hand on their back and push forward, gradually increasing the force, trying to push them. They must resist this force without moving their feet, see the pictures below. You will find that it becomes very hard to push them. As you increase the force, your SS receives information from its receptors and begins to adjust the muscle tension, joint rigidity, and weight distribution.
2.

3. Repeat the above procedure. This time as you apply the pressure, quickly release the force and then reapply it back and continue the push.

Your partner will now find it very hard to maintain his position, while you can push them with greater ease than before. What is occurring here is that your SS receives input from your body and makes adjustments to maintain its position. When the pressure is released suddenly, your SS registers the adjustment necessary to maintain balance and adjusts your body accordingly. When the pressure is immediately re-applied, it gets caught in its adjusting mode, which allows the body to be moved. The above explanation can be shortened to the term, "Muscle reassignment." (Chapél First introduced the above experiment & term, muscle reassignment).

Vestibular System

The vestibular system (VtS) has two primary roles: monitoring and adjusting the position of the head and working alongside the VS to control eye movement. Of interest here is its role in maintaining the position of the head. It is important for the body to maintain equilibrium, especially when moving to perform various stance changes and when propelling itself. The head has an ability to maintain itself when all other areas of the body are in a state of disconnection. The drunk staggering down the road is an example of this control. His body will not do as the mind commands and is all over the place, but in contrast his head is fairly stable. When a boxer gets tagged on the chin, his head wants to continue to fight but he's lost control of his legs and his body has abandoned all control, a TKO. The head is the one place where two systems used to control the body movements are located and are the last to shut down. A TKO is the shutting down of the SS by disrupting the nerve pathways that relay information from the receptors to the brain. The receptors for this system are found in the semicircular canals of the ear, lying in the temporal bone of the skull, just behind the organ that produces the sense of sound. This system is undetectable, though we might notice its existence when we become seasick or airsick. This system plays a vital role in maintaining the body balance and equilibrium when in motion. It is, along with the VtS, the gyroscope of the body. Tilting the head to one side can hamper the body's ability to right itself. If we control an attacker's head by manipulating it to the side and then locking it into this position so the head cannot reorient itself back to its normal position, then your attacker will find it very difficult to regain their posture and balance, as the main systems which keep the head in a state of equilibrium is being kept out of position. The head needs to be able to send signals to the rest of the body that it is now ready to right itself, but if the head is out of sync, then the rest of the body will follow.

Visual System

Apart from the obvious "being able to see," our eyes also process information about the environment and provide us with the orientation of objects surrounding us, including the location of our own limbs. This is due to the visual system (VS). This information takes the form of horizontal and vertical structures, such as doors, steps, walls, and enables our mind to navigate the body through the environment in which we find ourselves. The VS is also linked with the VtS to ensure that the body is kept in a state of equilibrium. We rely so heavily on the eyes that once they are closed or we are blinded, we become completely disoriented, yet as long as we are still and stable, the SS and the VtS can still maintain balance and posture. If we are blinded during movement, the whole body will struggle to regain its balance and posture. Thus in a fight situation, the benefits of taking someone's sight away are obvious. The VS also has built in reflexes protecting the body and head. If we are in a state of falling, the VtS along with the VS acts to keep the head upright. This is called the vestibulospinal reflex. The VS is one key to the startle reflex, the reflex that closes the eyes and pulls the head away from incoming danger. The direction of movement the heads takes when a punch is thrown and catches you unaware is backward and away from the incoming danger the head moves first and eventually the body catches up, this is a typical startle reflex in action.

All these reactions are initiated by information taken in by the VS, processed by the brain and conveyed to the muscles. The VS is also responsible for coordinating the information relayed to the brain through the SS in relation to where our limbs and body are in space and time. When the receptors in our fingers apply pressure to hold an object, the VS confirm the object and its position. If two people have hold of each other in a struggle, the forces acted upon the body and limbs can cause confusion as to where the mind believes the body to be. The result of a sudden change to an unexpected position can cause the body to lose balance and fall. In a specialised martial application, changing the position of limbs or effecting their orientation can cause the limbs to momentarily lose stability.

The parietal lobe is the area of the brain that receives all the sensory information sent by the Proprioceptive systems. It has complete control over all this sensory input and monitors the position and movement of all the body parts during every change we make. It is responsible for the creation of NMP and helps us learn movement from day one. Over the years it becomes such a part of the overall process that no attention is given to it. It's only when we start to learn new movements within sports for example, that we may discover that some moves are harder to learn than others. The reason for this is because they are out of balance with our natural NMP.

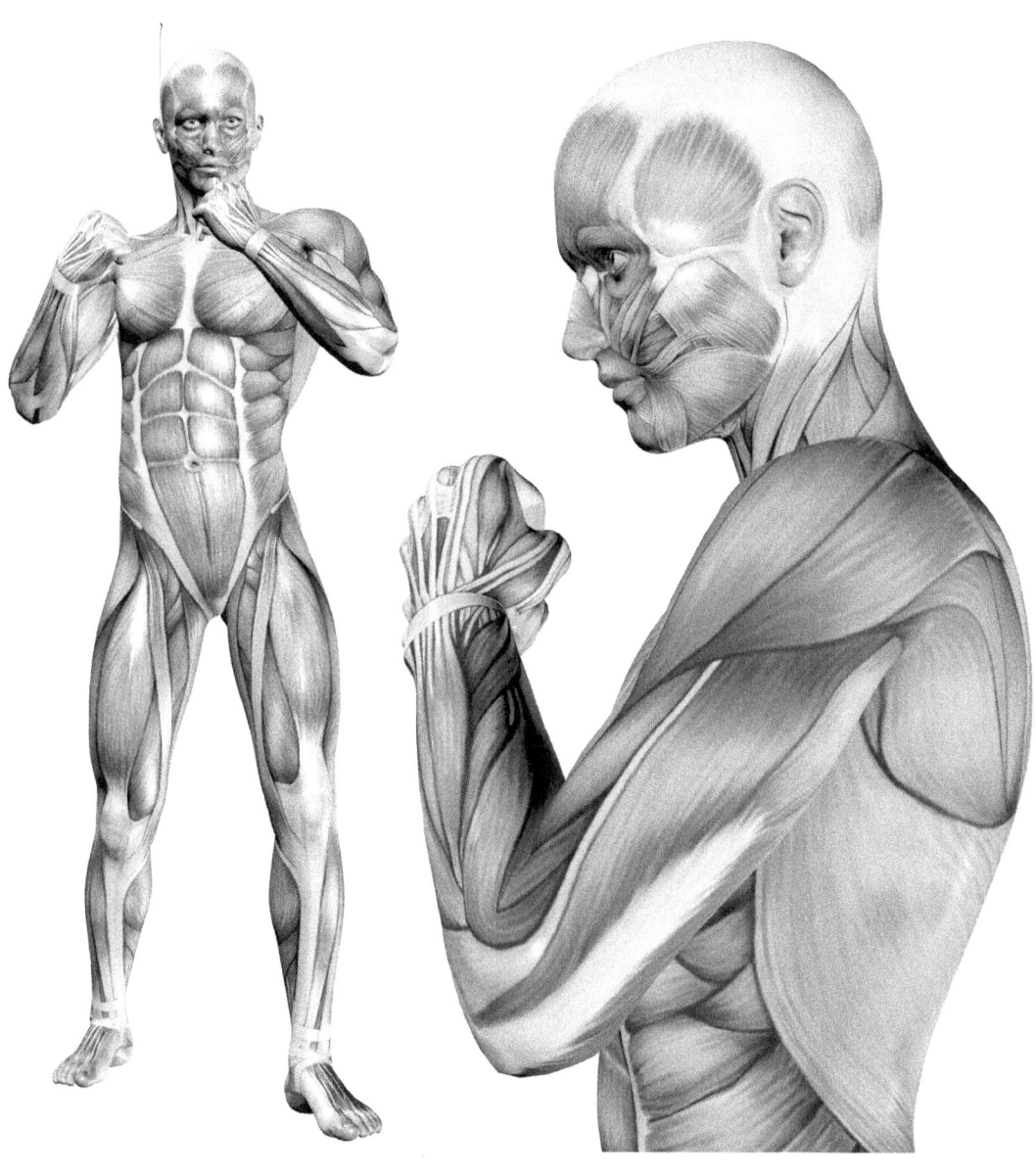

# 8 BIOMECHANICS OF THE BODY

This chapter delves into principles of physics; it will help explain how an understanding of these principles can help enhance techniques used within the martial arts. The human body is a complicated machine capable of extreme variations of movement; these principles will create a deeper understanding of mechanics.

SECTION 8.1

# LEVERS AND FULCRUMS

The majority of all movement created by our bodies is by way of a lever around a pivot point, called a fulcrum. Within the martial arts we are also able to apply these principles against our attacker. Understanding how these levers work is the first step to real-time application against a live attacker.

There are three classes of lever and each one exerts a different force when applied in a martial context. A first class lever is the most common in everyday living, such as the seesaw (the fulcrum being the centre point), or using a crow bar, when the fulcrum is closer to the resistance force. The longer the effort bar, the less force has to be applied to move the mass. A first class lever is also found within our musculoskeletal system in the agonist and antagonist muscles, when these muscles simultaneously act upon the opposite sides of a joint. The head balancing on the top of the spinal column is also an example of a first class lever.

To apply this type of lever in a martial context is relatively simple. If you position your attacker's arm over your shoulder with them behind you and their elbow pointing downwards so the arm does not bend naturally, have both your hands on their wrist and pull down a first class lever will result detailed in picture A below. The fulcrum point is your shoulder. If their elbow is directly on top of your shoulder, an equal amount of effort force needs to be applied by you to create movement in the resistance force (your attacker's body).

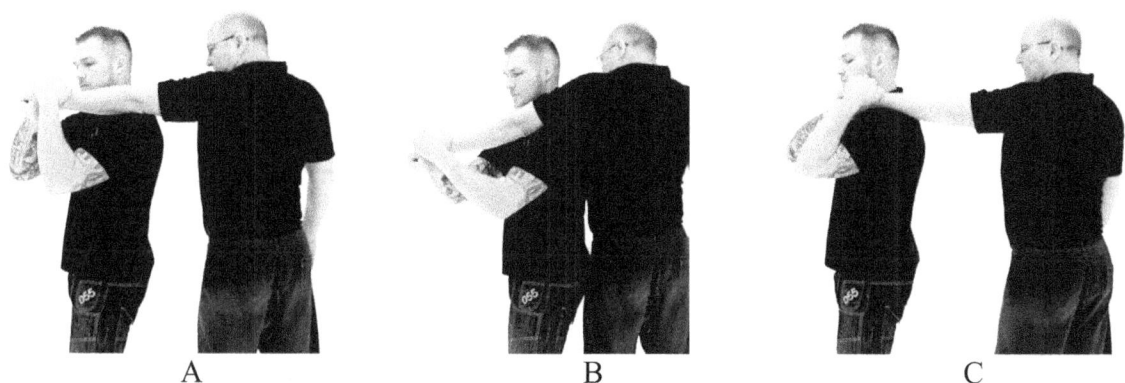

In this case, the load arm has an equal amount of distance either side of the fulcrum point. If the elbow is forward of your shoulder (PicB), creating a fulcrum point closer to the resistance force and effort force is applied, it will take much less effort to move the resistance force (their body) because the load arm has increased leverage. If the fulcrum is a reverse of this (PicC), then the effort must be considerably more.

When ground-working techniques are employed, like the well-known arm bar, with your opponent's arm between your legs, and you on your back with either one or both legs over your opponent, you are using the same first class lever. The difference is that you are applying a checking force to the resistance force and not allowing the lever to work, with the obvious aim of a submission.

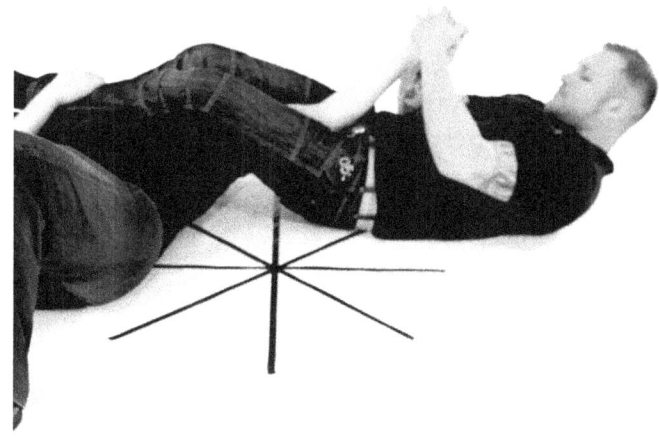

A second-class lever is found when both the resistance force and the effort force are the same side of the fulcrum. An example of this type of lever is a situation where you lift one end of a long heavy log off the ground, squatting down to take hold of the end and lift. The fulcrum is the point of the log still in contact with the ground, the resistance force is the weight of the log, and the effort force is your effort within your body to lift.

A second-class lever is seldom found within our musculoskeletal system. By standing naturally with all of your body stable, lift yourself up onto the balls of your feet, you have now in theory used a second-class lever. The resistance force is your body weight; the effort force is your muscles' ability to create enough effort against the resistance for you to lift up. The resistance force in this case is the amount of mass and the gravitational pull force exerted upon it.

This type of lever is not often used within a martial context because the movement is quite specialised. The scenario is one where your attacker has been thrown to the ground and you straddle their back with both feet on either side of their body, as in the pictures above. You reach down with both hands take hold of their chin and lift. Ultimately your attacker will come into contact with your legs before you get him too far off the floor, creating a first class lever, but the principle is the same as a class two lever.

The third class lever also has the effort force and the resistance force on the same side as the fulcrum. The difference is that the effort force acts in between the resistance force and the fulcrum. An example of this is a person holding a shovel: the resistance force is the weight of the content on the shovel, the fulcrum is the hand farthest away from the shovel, with the effort hand in between. This type of lever creates the majority of movement within our musculoskeletal systems. The design of this type of lever within the human body allows for a great amount of speed generation to occur. The effort force required to move a second-class lever is much greater than that of a third class lever, which helps explain our ability to move quickly.

A very simple example of a third class lever used in a martial context would be a rear naked choke or the last movement of a back fist strike.

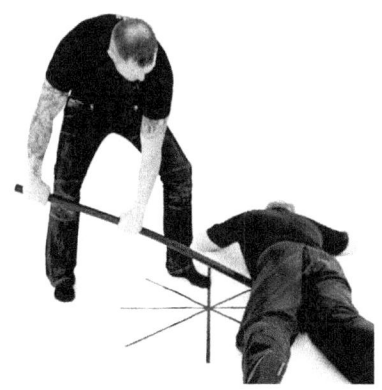 

SECTION 8.2

# MECHANISMS TO MOVE AGAINST MASS

Let's analyse the biomechanical movement required to allow you to move against another person's applied force, their body mass. The mechanism used in this movement has already been introduced in Chapter 2, section 2.5 in the experiments that enable you to feel the benefit of the skip mechanics.

Let's now look at this closer and at the martial application of the skip. While standing upright with both feet together, move the right foot back half a foot's length and bend both knees. When the right foot touches the ground, snap the leg straight. This action between the lower leg and the upper leg becomes that of a third class lever snapping open. As it does, it forces the upper body to move from its base. This type of propulsion can be initiated in any direction.

To apply this mechanism within a martial arts technique will depend on the situation that you need to move from. For example, standing still, you are caught from behind in an aggressive bear hug with your arms pinned. Just the aggression of the attack alone and the inertia the attacker brings with him will force your mass into movement. You will take steps forward until you come to rest. If you are caught off guard, you should find that your feet are still in the same position under your pelvic bone, and his next intention will be to lift you from the floor. To stop him lifting, we must apply a principle that will disrupt him. Let's assume you have managed to stop his lifting action. You now want to establish your base by stepping directly out to your left with your left foot. As you go to make the step, he feels your movement and prevents it. Now with full resistance being applied, take your right foot and step to your right about 200-300mm, just enough to give you a base to push from, bend your legs as above, and snap your right leg, using this mechanism to push in the direction you want to move, in this instance to the left. You are able to create a lot more force and move your attacker, which will help to stop his intention to lift, as you will have shifted your centre of mass. The quicker the skip mechanism is used, the more effective it becomes, so practice is required.

This biomechanical action is found in a multitude of situations where you either need to move against mass or to simply move quickly. It is not restricted to the martial arts, it can be found in all sports where quick mobile movements are required. Observe the rugby player in full sprint throwing a dummy and swaying his body first one way, and then another. If his foot leads the movement, the defender automatically picks it up.

The pictures below show the mechanism required to move against force.

SECTION 8.3

# ANATOMICAL BODY POSITIONING FOR RESISTING & PRODUCING FORCE

Being able to block an incoming strike at full power and being able to execute a strike with an aligned weapon so that you are at your most effective and do not cause injury to yourself are why correct anatomical body positions are extremely important. Within any strike where force is applied into an attacker, a proportional amount of the force will be redirected back into your own body through whichever weapon you have used, which then dissipates through your entire body.

I have already covered the application of anatomical alignment; so let's now look at a tackle technique. This is where your attacker tries to take you to the ground. They drop their shoulders, bend, then from a short distance away charge at you. If you stand your ground during the attack, once their mass comes into contact with your own, you will be driven back and in all likelihood taken to the ground. If you step back with either foot to form a brace without any substance or stability to back it up, then again you are likely to find yourself with dirt on your back.

As the impact is about to happen, you may well find yourself leaning into the attacker at the exact time that you perceive the impact will happen. This can be used to good effect as long as you make sure that the timing is correct. The action of stepping backwards and the need to create stability as you do so is important to enable you to resist a charging attacker.

Let's try two experiments designed to allow you to feel the effectiveness of the Platform Aligning Mechanism as described in section 2.1. There is an experiment to test the PAM when under constant pressure.

Let's repeat Experiment 1, but this time have the attacker try to tackle the defender instead of applying constant push force pressure. The key here is to find out that at the point of impact you are capable of creating a very stable platform to resist the contact. If you step back and PAM, then as contact occurs PAM again, you will increase the stability and your ability to resist the tackle. It is at this point that the body becomes rooted to the ground. (Experiments introduced by Chapél during seminars and classes.)

The sequence of pictures below, show the PAMing of the forward foot, just as your attacker's mass contacts your own.

The next step is to take this applied stability and use it to either resist force or apply force depending upon the situation at the split second in which either a block or a strike occurs. It's like firing a cannon ball from a cannon. If the cannon is on wheels with no means of stabilising the firing structure when the fuse is lit and the exchange of force happens, the cannon will recoil away from the cannon ball and as such, less force will be transferred into the ball. If the cannon is secured and stable, the majority of the force is transferred into the ball.

The same principles apply to any strike or block. If the body is not stable at the point of impact, any action will not be as effective as it could be if executed from a stable platform. The trick is to be able to shift from stability to mobility within a fight situation.

SECTION 8.4

# ANGLES OF DELIVERY

The angle in which you deliver any strike or block has a profound effect on the action of the attacker. It can cause the launching of another strike or the complete inability to respond. This is what is known as angle specifics. To look at this in more detail and to understand the specific paths of action, we must define the movement within a three dimensional construct. This is not an easy task, as we are taught many movements with only two dimensions.

In the art of Kenpo there is a symbolic symbol called the Universal Pattern (Parker (1987) Vol4). Using this base pattern, you can see the movement required much more easily. Being able to understand paths of movement in three dimensions is very important. The basics of angle specifics will give us a good understanding of how and why you may want to alter your angle of delivery.

For example, have a partner hold out his right arm directly in front of him, and with your left arm perform an inward block against the arm. The idea here is to observe the angle in which the arm is deflected. If your block is executed on a horizontal plain, the arm will be deflected along the same path. As this happens it may well trigger the movement of your partner's body. The harder the attack, the more movement there is in your partner. It may cause the whole body to twist and rotate, which may help your partner launch another weapon from the other side of his body. The path in which your arm travels, creates this reaction. The angle of delivery (Parker, jr. (1992) Encyclopedia of Kenpo) is from the point that you position your arm to start the move to the point where contact is made. The starting point is known as the point of origin.

If we now repeat the inward block and this time change the angle of delivery, which will also mean changing the point of origin, and attack the arm from a high zone, the reaction on your attacker's arm is going to be equal to the angle in which you have attacked the arm, driving the body downward toward the ground at an angle that causes his arm to cross his own body.

This type of action will restrict your partner's ability to be able to respond, as you will have caused his posture and body weight to shift. By knocking him off balance for a short period of time, you will diminish his ability to effectively respond until he re-establishes some of his posture and balance. If we look within the Universal Pattern, we can see these paths of travel. We all move from levers and as such the majority of paths of action are actually circular, even though I have described the above in terms of straight lines, orbital paths of action are used the most.

Blocks can be executed with either a straight-line angle of delivery or a circular orbital angle of delivery. It's important to understand these angles of delivery and how they change the effect on your attacker. Impact on the body and its effect is also a very important part of the understanding of angles of delivery. Taking a straight punch to the centre of the chest is another example to help illustrate the importance of these angles. If you stand directly in front of your partner and execute a straight punch, ensuring the angle of delivery is horizontal, the effect of the punch is going to hurt whatever happens. When hit in this manner, the body will move backwards from the force applied, since the force is being applied in a horizontal line. There is nothing to restrict the movement of the body in this direction, which is away from the incoming force.

Now change the angle of delivery so that the punch is downward. Now there is more mass to absorb the strike including the ground. Not having the freedom to move back without restriction causes a greater amount of damage on your attacker. The change in the angle of delivery will drive the weight towards the ground rather than directly away as in the first example. The hands have the ability to change angles of delivery at will. Look at the Universal Pattern represented as a sphere and all the possible paths of action that can be taken. The angles of delivery are also numerous.

SECTION 8.5

# TORQUE

Torque is one of the three main principles for producing power through our body. Let's look at torque and isolate which parts of our body can use this principle within a martial application.

To create any type of torque force within our body, there has to be an applied action. In the case of torque, this action is created by the movement of our muscles around and upon our skeletal structure. When a force causes rotation, the rotation occurs about an axis point. Torque is not actually a force but the result of forces applied around this axis point. Any type of force that is applied to the body can create torque. While standing with your feet together and being pushed on your left shoulder, this applied force creates rotational movement around the centre line of your body and so produces torque on the body. When we rotate our hand while opening a doorknob, we rotate our forearm muscle around the ulna and radius, and the resulting action in the hand is rotational torque. Torque can also be produced around the hip axis, such as when we rotate the right hip just before we execute a right reverse punch. While the punch is traveling along its path of action, rotate the fist around the forearm bones. We now have different stages of torque connecting with each other to create a more effective punch, and the end result is a different effect acting upon the human body.

The following pictures show the effects of torque when force is applied to one side of your body.

The resulting effect that torque has on the human body is not obvious. The human body mostly consists of water, applying a punch without torque will still have the effect of vibration within the body. Torque of the fist on impact will also create this vibrational kinetic wave, this time however the effect will be spiraling as well. The result will be a dissipation of energy that feels distinctly different from a punch without torque.

SECTION 8.6

# LAW OF INERTIA

An object either still or moving will remain in that state until a force is applied upon it. If the object is still, it will require a force greater than its mass to change its current state. If an object is moving in a straight line, it will continue on this line at a constant speed until an external force is applied against it, but will not require a large amount of force to alter its direction.

The following pictures show the application of inertia on a committed punch, when redirection occurs.

There are constant forces acting upon us, gravity being the most obvious, but there is also friction. In applying this law to biomechanical movement, it is apparent that inertia will not work in its literal terms, since we have control over the forces that we produce, unless we are falling out of control. However, the theory is very useful in understanding movements within the martial arts, 'Every body continues in its state of rest, or of uniform motion in a straight line, unless it is compelled to change that state by forces applied on it' Hamill, phd, Knutzen, phd. (2009).

Let's look at a couple of ways to apply the understanding of the Law of Inertia in a martial context. If your attacker launches a lunging punch at you, he will bring a certain amount of inertia with this lunge. If he has committed this action fully, he will, for a time, be just like an object moving with inertia and unable to alter direction. If at this time you were able to execute a parrying motion to the fist, then you would be adhering to the Law of Inertia. As you alter his line of movement, you won't need a large amount of force within your parry to affect the large amount of force and inertia being applied by your attacker.

Moving a large person who is stable and still is another scenario and unless you have a greater amount of force to bring to bear on that person, you will not move them. Not only do you have to overcome his weight, you also have to deal with the power contained within his musculoskeletal structure. If they are fit and strong, you will have a hard job starting their inertia. That's where weakening strikes and pain comes into play.

SECTION 8.7

# EFFECTS OF GRAVITY

Gravity is a force we are all familiar with, as it is very easy to see the effects of this force in the world. The famous apple falling from a tree was the catalyst for Newton's theory that any object, when released from a height or propelled into the air, will fall to the ground unless it has enough force to leave the earth's atmosphere.

From those early days when we first learned to stand on our own two feet and even as a young infant laid in our cot, we were under the force of gravity until our muscles grew strong enough to lift our bodies clear off the ground and walk. We grew and developed with gravity every day of our lives and unless we are one of a lucky few astronauts, we will never experience a day without this force acting upon our body. The force created by gravity is known as non-contact force. The body's weight is a direct consequence, resulting from the amount of mass and acceleration applied on the body due to gravity. This means that the body weight is in fact a force in itself and as such it has a line of action and a point of application.

The following pictures show an upright posture and a posture that is out due to the leaning of the upper mass forward.

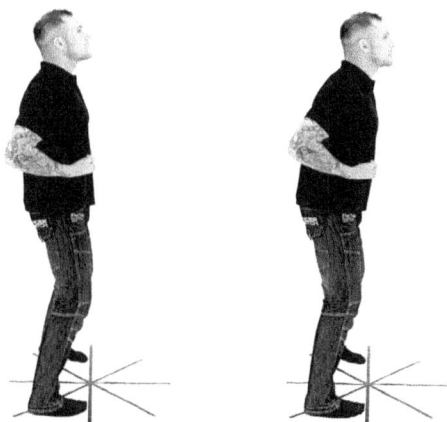

The body's point of gravity is known as the centre of gravity. These two terms are interchangeable. In the Orient this is called the Ti Ten point. This point is only the centre of gravity while the body is in balance with an erect posture. When you lean over, the centre of gravity will shift. When you allow the supporting leg muscles to relax and bend, gravity takes over and the body accelerates towards the ground. The legs are the only supporting limbs allowing you to resist gravity; it is this constant force that the body has to resist every day.

To use this force to your advantage within the martial arts, you must coordinate the relaxing and the re-engaging of your legs at the same instant that you time your strikes. If this can be achieved, then the natural force of gravity is used to enhance the effectiveness of your strikes.

The following pictures give an example of gravity being used to increase the effectiveness of your strikes.

Performing an inward overhead downward elbow to an attacker's back is an ideal example of how you can employ this force to your advantage. Just before the impact of the elbow, disengage your leg muscles and then reengage them again. At that precise moment, your body mass will be part of your weapon rather than just the amount of force you can deliver by just using your arm. Executing any strike in this manner uses the body's weight as part of the delivery platform.

The next part of this formula is to also use the force of inertia to further improve the power generated. The majority of your strikes can use a combination of these two forces, while rotational torque will cause a different type of collision and affect upon your attacker.

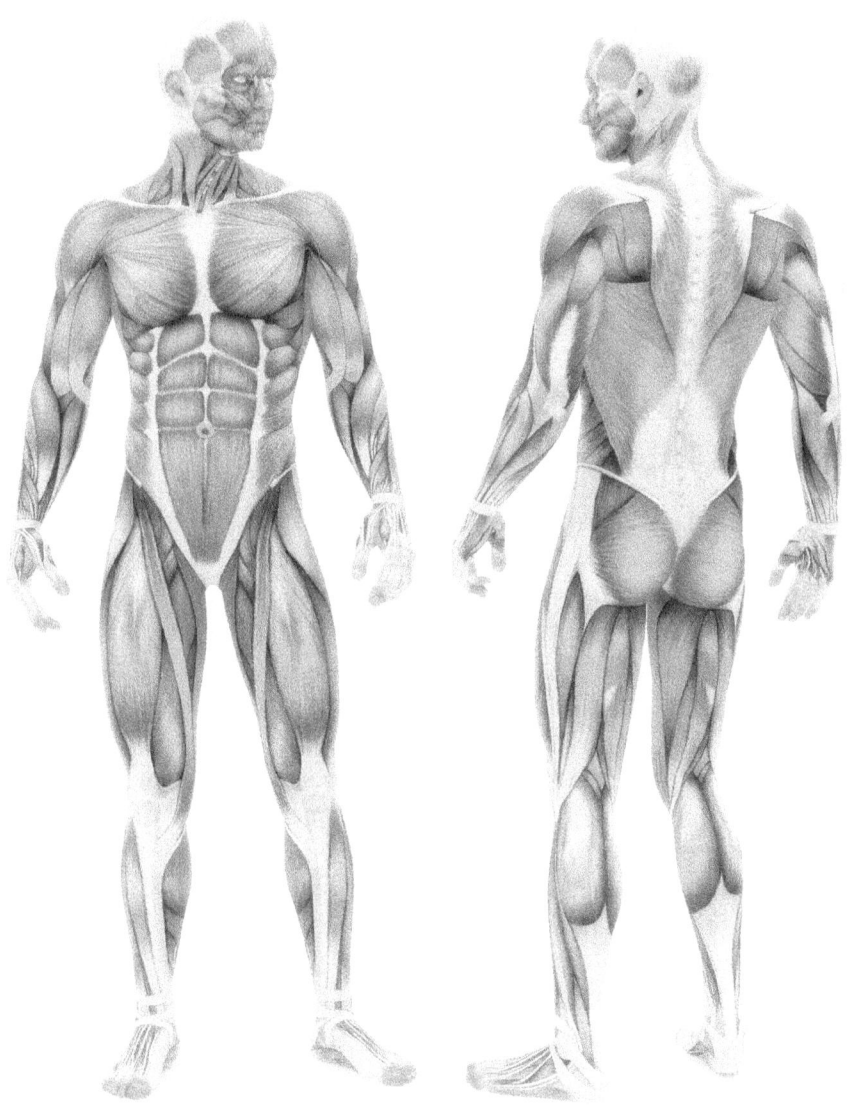

# 9 ACTION – REACTION

Martial arts techniques often require participant interaction. Having an understanding of natural body reactions and reflexes will help in designing and teaching techniques.

SECTION 9.1

# FORCE APPLIED

Possibly one of the least looked at and misunderstood areas of the martial arts is force applied. When it comes down to the application of force against another human being, there are as many ways to react, as there are to apply the force. Some schools of thought that train for a one or two strike fight totally commit themselves to destroying their attacker with the first blow; there is no concern that the technique will not work. There are those which use a multiple striking system, moving from one strike to another with no concern that even one of their strikes have worked. What is important is to have an understanding of applied force, action-reaction, and the understanding of this principle when applied to the body. We are all made differently and we all react in different ways to varying amounts of pain, so how can force be analysed?

Let's look at some of the detail contained within force applied. There are two applications of the force applied theory. One is applied to a linear line of force and the other to the angular line. In linear, the law states that, "For every torque exerted by one body on another body, there is an equal and opposite torque exerted by the latter body on the former." Hamill, phd. Knutzen, phd. (2009). Forces never act in isolation. There are always two parts to this equation: the force exerted by one object on another is equal to the force exerted by the object receiving the initial force back to the object generating that force. The exchanges of forces between two objects are also equal in magnitude and opposite in direction.

In applying this process to the martial arts, we've already seen a few examples of having a stable base to launch your weapons from. When your force hits another body an equal and opposite reaction will occur. If this were the case, then every time a person hits another, they will affect their own body as well as their attackers.

We know from experience that is not the case. The difference lies in the literal translation of objects and forces. We can apply a large amount of force as a human and, to a degree, the force applied law causes the same forces to act in the way described. We are also built of flesh and bone, thus the body absorbs the forces we are capable of transmitting as contact is made and the forces exchanged.

We also have a tendency to move away from danger or pain. It is not realistic to perform martial arts moves on another person and not consider reaction. If an attacker throws a punch, which is blocked, and then a counter is applied, to have the attacker still standing with his punch held out in the air is simply not logical.

This type of practice can have a very detrimental effect on your thought process and your actions. Your move says that your technique has not worked, since your attacker is still standing there like a statue. It is more logical and practical to assume that your technique has worked and that the attacker will react in a certain prescribed fashion. If this happens, you will have action-reaction, this then has to be applied to a combat situation.

The next trick is knowing that when your strike or technique works, what will be the reaction of your attacker? This is where the psychology of confrontation comes in. Having knowledge of this area allows you to logically look at the potential responses from your attacker.

You will also need to have a good understanding of your body's natural defence mechanisms, including startle and pain reflexes. There are some instances within a martial application when the law of action-reaction is closer to physics than it is to the body reacting to a pain stimulus.

There may be an occasion when pain simply does not register with an attacker, such as when under the influence of drugs or alcohol. If you rely on a pain stimulus for the success of your technique, you may be in trouble. The body has a great ability to absorb impact. Witness a person getting hit by a car and then standing up and walking away; the force and density of the car brings a large amount of magnitude to the impact and causes a massive action-reaction, but what you do not see, is the force from the body being redirected back into the car.

A great deal of force and magnitude must be behind a punch to create a massive action-reaction on an attacker. Applying some of these principles and theories will give you a good chance of a successful outcome to any encounter. This is one reason why backup mass is so important in creating power or a greater magnitude behind the strike.

Let's look at how this works when a body hits another body. Imagine you are standing there minding your own business when an attacker comes from behind you and applies a bear hug. When he moves in to engage you and applies the attack, he brings a certain amount of force. His body is moving and has inertia. When his body hits your body, the law of action-reaction goes into effect. Your body and mass will move, but a certain amount of the collision force will be redirected back into the attacker's body. Since your mass was still and assuming that his mass is equal to or in excess of yours, then when contact occurs, you will move. If his mass is a lot less than yours, then the inertia needed to move you has to be greater than his mass. If he is a great deal heavier than you, then less inertia is needed. Action-reaction is therefore relative to weight.

When training this type of attack in a school environment, introducing inertia to the technique is often left out. The attacker comes at you and then stops and attacks from a stable position behind you with no intent used. If you intensify the attack by bringing inertia into the scenario, it will change the defence tactics, as the defender will have to first survive the action-reaction state before he can move to the defence, which is suitable for the attack.

Surviving the initial assault (Chapél (1991) Course book 101Y) is one of the very first and most important parts of any defence technique. Looking at it in another way, it is surviving the force brought by your attacker before any significant action can be applied to your attacker, unless of course you can anticipate the attack. That is why understanding action-reaction is such an important part of any martial encounter. There are only two major principles in applied force within movement and striking: inertia, or mass being used to create penetration on a horizontal plane, and gravity, or mass being used to create penetration on a vertical plain. In either of these, a big difference will occur if the weapon used to deliver the force is large or small. The surface contact area will also play a part in the effectiveness of any strike. If these principles are applied and the weapon used is the shoulder, a big reaction will happen. What this will not give you is a specific injury, as the surface area in contact with the attacker is too large. If the weapon used is the point of the elbow with the same degree of inertia and gravitational force, the result is far more effective. The surface area in contact with the attacker is concentrated and therefore the amount of pressure exerted through the contact point is far greater. As a result, trauma is more likely to occur.

Force applied is a subject all in itself. I encourage martial artists to study these principles and the effects they cause, including the medical implications of effective strikes. There is so much more to action-reaction than meets the eye.

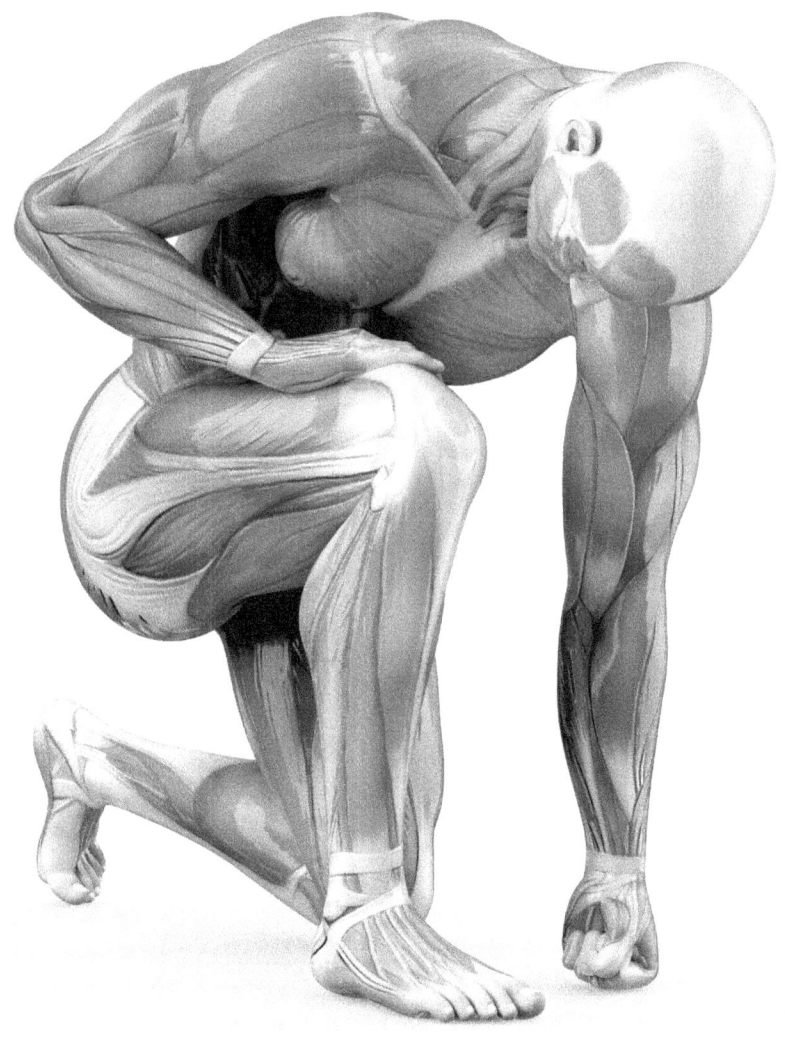

# REFERENCES

Parker, E, K. Infinite insights into Kenpo, 2 Physical Analysation (1983). Delsby publications.

Parker, jr. Ed Parker's Encyclopedia of Kenpo, (1992) Ed Rolph,D. Delsby publications.

Chapel, R. Phd, 'Martial Science University' (1991) course book S-101 (Y).

Parker, E, K. Infinite insights into Kenpo, 5 Mental & Physical Applications (1983). Delsby publications.

Parker, E, K. Infinite insights into Kenpo, 4 Physical & Mental Constituents, (1983). Delsby publications.

Hamill, J, phd. & Knutzen, K, M, phd. Biomechanical basis of human movement. 'Linear Kinetics' (2009) Third Edition, (1995) Williams & Wilkins, a Wolters Kluwer business.

For all those who seek knowledge, I encourage you to train with anyone you can, seek out knowledge and always push your own personal boundaries. It is here in the realm of challenges that life bears it's meaning. Understanding yourself is sometimes the hardest thing to find.

## **Grant me**

Grant me, truthful knowledge, when I search my soul inside

Not to uncover false dreams upon which we can become relied.

But I ask you to guide me, in asking the right questions and finding the key to unlock the honest power of truth, long forgotten from memory

Grant me, expanding intellect when I look outside of myself at the unknown

Not to make me blind and deaf to everything my senses know

But to give me a sense of courage, a direction and a force travelling through all the difficult times pointing out the wisest course

Grant me, humble wisdom, when I search the words I use

Not to stumble upon thoughts and actions and looks that can be misconstrued

But to speak a true and steady tongue which is able to teach and calm, and keep all of those dear to me safe and away from harm

Grant me, loyal kindness as I share this journey of knowledge contained

Not to make judgements on others or be ignorant of experiences others have gained

But to simply shake their hand and point my way to impart these values and learning of mine and be content in the thought that these words printed will cascade through time.

Leah-Marie Mills

## ABOUT THE AUTHOR

The Author has been a key figure in the martial arts and combative arena for over 30 years and during this time has developed an extensive knowledge of psychology and biomechanical applications within this field.

'The Secret Science of Modern Martial Arts' is essential study material for any person seeking to expand their knowledge and skills of biomechanics and movement during physical confrontation. This fundamental text offers those with open minds the opportunity to gain an understanding of human movement and how this translates into practice. Within this book you will find the keys to understanding such areas as movement, biomechanics of the body, propulsion, neuromuscular programming and power principles of strikes, to name but a few.

www.ingramcontent.com/pod-product-compliance
Lightning Source LLC
Chambersburg PA
CBHW080613230426
43664CB00019B/2881